Get Set for Teacher Training

Titles in the GET SET FOR UNIVERSITY series:

Get Set for Teacher Training

Don Skinner

Edinburgh University Press

© Don Skinner, 2005

Edinburgh University Press Ltd
22 George Square, Edinburgh

Typeset in Sabon
by Servis Filmsetting Ltd, Manchester, and
printed and bound in Finland by
WS Bookwell

A CIP record for this book is available from the British Library

ISBN 0 7486 2139 3 (paperback)

CONTENTS

ACKNOWLEDGEMENTS

I would like to acknowledge the very real way in which discussions with family, colleagues in the University of Edinburgh and other academic contacts have helped me clarify the ideas presented in this book.

1 INTRODUCTION

If you are reading this you are probably considering, or are about to begin, a teacher training course. I expect you want to know more about what such a course will be like, gain some insight into the demands it will make, and be offered some advice on how to do well on it. This book aims to provide exactly that and so help you make a successful start to a career in teaching.

Teaching is a career that many people find very satisfying. They are aware of playing a valuable social role, enjoy interacting with young people and are rewarded by seeing them develop and learn. They are enthusiastic about the subjects they teach and seek ways of getting others interested in these subjects. British society has high expectations of its schools and consequently debates on educational issues and school performance results are closely followed. Of course, schools by themselves can't be expected to do everything; but they do have a key role in developing knowledge and skills, social awareness, healthy lifestyles, and informed and active citizens. Teaching has opened up and developed significantly in recent years, providing an increasing range of professional roles. There are, of course, plenty of challenges which are best met by an approach to teaching that is at once positive and realistic. It is just such an approach that this book seeks to adopt.

There are several kinds of training courses, and different routes to becoming a teacher, but they all have a great deal in common. All teachers in training need to find out about how to succeed on teaching placements, plan lessons, manage classrooms, write educational assignments and apply insights from developmental psychology. All need to learn how to meet the nationally determined standards of professional knowledge,

1

understanding and skill. This guide introduces you to these common concerns. It also attends to the distinctive needs of its varied readers – intending primary and secondary teachers, those embarking on undergraduate, postgraduate and school-based courses, those training in England, Scotland, Wales and Northern Ireland. In the UK overall, of the present total of some 40,000 entrants, the proportions training for primary and for secondary teaching are roughly equal, and the split between the undergraduate and postgraduate routes is also more or less even. An excellent variety of courses exists and arrangements can be found to suit different interests, needs and circumstances.

If you are still considering whether to become a teacher, I hope this book will help you make a more informed decision through the picture it provides of what teacher training is like, of its challenges and satisfactions, and of what is required from teachers today. If you are reading this as a student taking Education Studies as part of another degree you should find it helps you understand a classroom teacher's perspective on educational issues (a perspective often downplayed in books on Education Studies) and you should find highly relevant the chapters on psychological and sociological perspectives and the whole of Part III on study skills.

This book gives you an idea of how teacher training programmes are organised and what tutors, schools and assessors are looking for. It shows you how to fight quickly through educational jargon, link theory and practice, and exploit your preferred learning style. It emphasises the importance of having a life outside teaching, taking care of your personal health, and learning how to avoid becoming stressed and how to build confidence in using information technology as a teacher. With its advice about how to think around the difficult areas, controversies and debates in education, it offers a framework for making sense of reading and of experience in schools. It identifies the kinds of skills you need to develop.

In taking up teaching you are joining entrants from all walks of life. Many have somehow known early on, in school or university, that they definitely wanted to teach. They have therefore focused their career planning firmly on this, opting for either an undergraduate course like the BEd or a degree followed by a one-year postgraduate training. But nowadays many others – among them police officers, marketing managers, artists, scientists, even deep-sea divers – switch careers to become teachers. This wide range of backgrounds and experiences enriches the profession. It is also worth noting that teaching in the UK is becoming a more open career with people moving out into other occupations as well as into it from them. The plain fact is that teaching develops important 'transferable skills' like organisation, management and communication. These are skills that are widely sought.

As a teacher you will find yourself in some notable company. Did you know that Schubert trained as a teacher? So did several politicians and other public figures. A number of philosophers and also poets and playwrights, including very possibly Shakespeare himself, have at one time held teaching positions.

I hope you will find this book a handy reference throughout your studies, but it does not aim to be a comprehensive textbook of the kind you might still expect to find if you were taking up, say, economics or chemistry at university. In studying to become a teacher there is certainly a good deal of reading to do, along with planning, practising and discussing teaching. But the most useful reading is spread throughout a variety of books and articles, ranging from practical classroom guides, to official policy documents, to deeper theoretical studies and reports of research. Teacher training is not a matter of 'mugging up' set knowledge from a series of course textbooks, as you might find in medicine or law.

In writing up assignments and preparing for teaching placements you will be expected to make use of a range of sources on topics such as developmental psychology, teaching and learning, information technology, curriculum, and wider professional roles. This guide should help you understand the issues you will face and main ideas you are likely to encounter, and help you decide what to read and how to get the most out of it. Its glossary of key terms and acronyms, which one tends to meet unexpectedly without a clear definition close at hand, should also prove useful for quick reference.

This book also offers practical advice on how to handle the nuts and bolts of a teacher training course. It covers how to make good relations with teachers in schools, negotiate with your tutor, build a network of support among your fellow students, and develop the study skills to enable you to tackle your various assignments smoothly and with genuine satisfaction. When you are facing the ups and downs of placement, or are finding reading for assignments difficult, this book shows you how you can succeed and make a good start to teaching.

STRUCTURE OF THE BOOK

The various topics included in this volume can be explored in whatever order suits your particular needs and interests. For convenience, however, it has been organised into the three distinct parts into which the topics seem naturally to fall.

Part I is about studying education. It includes ideas about teaching and learning, curriculum and assessment, insights from developmental psychology and the study of the school in the context of the educational system as a whole and the wider society. In short, it gives you an insight into how to approach the theory and practice of education.

Properly relating theory to practice in education is always a challenge and some problems undoubtedly persist. But significant developments have occurred and you can now confidently expect that theory and practice are effectively brought together on your course and focused firmly on the teacher's classroom role. Most books and courses draw out implications for professional action in schools and classrooms from the ideas, theories and research evidence they discuss. This guide shows how to make such links yourself and also draws attention to the fact that linking theory and professional action is often far from being a simple process of direct application. The relationship between ideas, evidence and practice in education, as in other related fields, is inevitably more complicated. This is because questions of conflicting aims and values also arise, and because context is so important in teaching. Understanding all this will help you to look critically at both theory and practice. You need both to be a good teacher, and you should be aware that the ability to link theory and practice intelligently is one of the hallmarks of professionalism. Your training will also cover wider professional responsibilities and understanding in a way that should help you develop a professional perspective, and eventually a voice, on national educational policy issues.

Part II focuses squarely on professional practice. It covers learning on placement, teaching skills and the issue of learning styles, the wider responsibilities of teachers beyond classroom teaching, how to use and develop subject knowledge and how to take charge of your own continuing development as a teacher. (This includes undertaking a classroom research project, something often expected towards the end of a course.) Initial teacher education can no longer be seen as a once-for-all preparation for a career. Teaching is rapidly developing not only through mounting research evidence, theoretical studies, and debate and policy development but also through the impact that information and communications technology (ICT) is having on teaching and learning, school organisation and links to the world outside school.

Part III deals with relevant aspects of what are often called study skills. Really they are much more than that. They are transferable skills and professional communication skills for the teacher's day-to-day role and for continuing professional development; they are not just skills for getting through a course. After considering broad approaches to study, learning from lectures and reading educational theory and research reports are discussed. Further chapters consider writing effective assignments, preparing and giving presentations on aspects of teaching, and managing your time effectively. The last two can make a big difference to professional confidence and help you feel in control.

The key role of universities in teacher education is to

develop deep understanding and critical analysis of ideas, issues and practices, and awareness of the findings and role of educational research in developing education and teaching. Not all students find these aspects easy at first and so this aspect has been emphasised and illustrated at appropriate points throughout this book.

WHAT IS INVOLVED IN A TEACHER TRAINING COURSE?

There are three main ingredients in most standard teacher education courses: curriculum studies, education studies and placement. Let's consider each briefly in turn.

Curriculum studies in courses at undergraduate level will typically aim to develop good subject understanding. In some courses this will be combined with the study of appropriate teaching methods so that 'Mathematics' or 'Language' will not just be the academic study of mathematics or language but also how to teach these subjects to a particular age range of pupils. In other courses there will be academic study of core subjects like English, Mathematics and Biology while another part of the degree programme (say 'Primary Teaching' or some Education Studies module) will include discussion of teaching methods. If you are on a postgraduate secondary programme, you will already have acquired deep subject knowledge. Hence the emphasis in curriculum study will naturally be on considering how to teach your subject – Art and Design, Geography, English or whatever – to the range of secondary school learners. The role of secondary school examinations will also figure prominently here. Postgraduate primary courses try to steer carefully between offering some basic subject knowledge on topics which students may not have studied at university and explaining teaching approaches to these subjects.

The second ingredient, education studies, shows considerable variation. Many courses have a series of education studies modules. In some places the term used is 'professional studies' and this is clearly separated from teaching methods. In other courses, professional studies and general methods are deliberately integrated in a central course component on 'theory and practice of teaching'. Whatever the arrangement, the aim is usually to undertake sustained study of educational issues and themes, linked to consideration of implications for professional action.

The pattern of teaching placements also varies considerably across teacher education courses. Many BEd courses will have placements in each year of the programme, with longer placements towards the end of the course. In Scotland (where such courses last four years) there might be a five-week placement in years one and two and a ten-week placement in years three and four. In the UK, postgraduate courses are usually thirty-six weeks long. In Scotland half the time is spent on placement. In England, Wales and Northern Ireland it can be two thirds. Over a course a student might experience three or four different schools. Some have long placements in one or two schools, prioritising the benefits of in-depth experience over variety of contexts. School-based courses and alternative routes place even more emphasis on learning to teach in school settings and have fewer educational essays to write.

MEETING THE PROFESSIONAL STANDARDS

In order to gain a teaching qualification, students on all teacher education courses in the UK have to meet a set of nationally determined professional standards. A 'standard' is a statement of the expected outcomes of teacher education. It specifies the knowledge and understanding, skills and professional values teachers are expected to be able to demonstrate by the end of the course.

Until a few years ago teacher education outcomes were set out as lists of expected 'competences' and you will still find the term competences used in books, articles and official statements in some parts of the UK. But the general trend has been to replace 'competences' with 'standards.' Standards have a broader connotation than competences (often interpreted as involving narrow technical skills) and are thus better suited to the more creative, flexible and open phase teaching is beginning to experience.

The specification of standards varies within the UK with its devolved responsibilities for educational policy. Each country naturally likes to put its own particular stamp on statements of educational aims and standards. The differences can be instructive. Comparative educational study can be a stimulating aid to thinking critically about education, the shock value of seeing that other countries do things differently challenging the assumption that the way things are done here represents some law of nature. In education, as elsewhere, there is more than one good way of doing things, each with its particular strengths and weaknesses. What will best suit a particular system will depend very much on the particular cultural, political and other features of its context.

Along with some differences of expression and particular national emphases, however, a basic similarity in content and purpose in teacher training standards can be detected across the UK. This also reflects a global trend to set out expected outcomes for public services like education, medicine and social work and for 'performance management'. This emphasises features such as outcome specifications, evidence-based training, accountability and, more controversially, performance-related pay. Alongside policies generated locally, developments from around the world influence practice in UK schools. Many industrialised countries find themselves wrestling with quite similar problems, albeit in distinctive contexts.

In England and Wales the standards set out what is required to achieve Qualified Teacher Status, commonly called QTS standards. In Scotland everyone talks about the Standard for Initial Teacher Education or the ITE benchmark standards. In Northern Ireland the term competences is still used and the key idea is that of 'eligibility to teach', with conditions being laid down about acceptable qualifying courses. In England the QTS standards are grouped as follows:

- professional values and practice;
- knowledge and understanding;
- teaching.

The Welsh version is very similar and takes account of the Welsh cultural and linguistic context. In Scotland the Standard for Initial Teacher Education is seen as an interacting triangle of:

- profession knowledge and understanding;
- professional skills;
- professional values and personal commitment.

This is clearly very close to the English and Welsh pattern but in Scotland the integrated nature of these aspects of professional development is strongly emphasised.

In the English and Welsh standards, a broad category like Teaching is divided into:

- planning;
- monitoring and assessment;
- teaching and class management.

At the most detailed level (taking as an example the standard for class management in England) they look like this (Teacher Training Agency 2002):

- They know a range of strategies to promote good behaviour and establish a purposeful learning environment.
- They set high expectations for pupils' behaviour and establish a clear framework for classroom discipline to anticipate and manage pupil behaviour constructively and promote self-control and independence.

In Scotland it is stated clearly that such specifications are not to be regarded as a list of isolated competences. The Scottish approach also gives emphasis to critical reflection on the school system and being able to articulate and justify educational arguments and practices. In England and Wales perhaps more emphasis can be detected on presenting curriculum knowledge to learners, handling their misconceptions and ensuring that cultural differences among pupils from our ethnically diverse society are properly taken into account.

Teachers, teacher educators and schools have found specifying standards useful in several ways. Research studies claim that they provide strong motivation, clear, practical guidance, a regard for evidence and professional satisfaction (Reeves et al. 2002). However the standards approach has many critics who express strong concern about the 'performance management' approach. They argue that this can lead to stress, demotivation and equity issues and question its underlying political ideology and economic assumptions. They advocate instead a broader approach based on critical engagement with the educational, economic and social control issues underlying the standards debate and a greater degree of professional autonomy for teachers.

Alex Moore (2000) has pointed out three different ways of thinking about teachers that you may find easy to grasp and interesting to follow up as you go through your course and think about the standards. These are the charismatic teacher, the competent teacher and the reflective teacher. Let us consider each of them briefly.

First there is the charismatic teacher who teaches well largely through force of personality and apparently inborn teaching skills and qualities of character. He or she is able to command enthusiasm, respect and commitment, clearly cares for the pupils and aims to make a difference in their lives. This may be an attractive vision but it seems to assume that you either have it or you don't and that training won't make much difference. A second conception is that of the competent teacher who masters the standards through systemic training. This includes training in lesson planning, class management, core teaching skills like explaining and questioning, assessment methods and reporting, and communication with parents. Emphasis is also placed on having a good grasp of subject knowledge and how to present it. Acquiring these skills is seen as the main function of training; and teaching is interpreted as applying these clearly defined skills to help pupils learn. In the same way, from this perspective school learning is taken to mean achievement of the various government-specified learning targets and outcomes.

But school learning is surely more than this and not so easily pinned down. The trouble is that the competence approach can become narrow and fragmented, riding carelessly over the value issues and broad aims at the heart of teaching. For example, class management is not just about somehow controlling children, whatever the cost in class atmosphere and teacher-pupil relationships. To be sure, we need a system that actually achieves order in class; but not just any system. From an educational perspective, class management is about helping children develop self-discipline, an understanding of co-operation, social order and effective personal relationships. We need a broad view of these educational aims and values and of how to foster children's personal and social development. The competence approach can lead to lack of creativity and a rather mechanical application of supposed general teaching skills to the neglect of a more open and flexible approach whereby teachers learn to adjust aims and teaching to contexts, stages and subjects.

A third concept is that of the reflective practitioner. This places strong emphasis on critical self-evaluation. Reflective practitioners develop teaching by reflecting carefully on their own practice, engaging in dialogue with colleagues, and learning from research and other studies of education. From this perspective, teaching looks more like an art than a science, taking more account of the messy complexity of the classroom and the role of intuitive judgement. Some educationists hope through this 'reflective practice' approach to reclaim teaching from bureaucrats, politicians and the competence discourse and revive a more rounded conception of the teacher's role and educational aims. Carr (2003) however cautions that the notion of the reflective teacher is too narrow and that it frequently reduces to just another version of 'applied theory.' An approach, he argues, that is misjudged because it neglects the value-laden issues and essentially moral questions at the heart of educational debates. Moore (2000) suggests that the reflective practice approach can become too inward-looking with much self-blame. The locus of any necessary change tends to be viewed as the individual rather than raising the question of broader social policy changes and issues in the wider society. He goes on to argue for a 'reflexive' not just a reflective approach. This involves looking closely at one's own developmental history as a teacher to aid deeper understanding of educational issues and the teacher's role.

To sum up, although the very basis of the professional standards approach is hotly debated, standards are something all teachers have to meet and come to terms with. The point is that there are different ways of doing this. Worthwhile professional development involves gradually gaining a critical understanding of such issues and learning to make your own judgement about how to respond to these debates in your work as a teacher.

EDUCATION AS AN ACADEMIC DISCIPLINE

One good way to develop thinking further is to consider just what kind of study education involves. The exact nature of education as a subject or discipline is still a matter of dispute among educational writers, however. It does not seem to be a single academic discipline like history or psychology or biology and is perhaps best seen as a broad area of study to which ideas from different traditional disciplines contribute. Psychology, sociology, and philosophy, it is widely recognised, all contribute in an important way to educational thinking. Perhaps, then, education is more like medicine (which draws on anatomy, physiology, biochemistry) or engineering (which draws on for example physics, and mechanics). Yet education does not seem to be quite as clearly related to its contributory disciplines as medicine is to anatomy or engineering to mechanics. Anatomy and mechanics are hard sciences with established bodies of knowledge and clear applications. The disciplines that contribute to educational studies, however, are not hard sciences with generally agreed research procedures and established bodies of knowledge. In fact the aims and methods of psychology and sociology are much in debate and the relationships of findings from these areas to educational practice appears much less direct or obvious than the applications of physiology to medicine or physics to engineering.

Education is certainly an applied field, not just a pure academic study. What have come to be called the 'practical theories' or professional 'craft knowledge' of working teachers – the know-how developed through thoughtful experience in educational settings – has now been recognised by educationists as a valid and important aspect of educational study. Much of this is tacit knowledge, unspoken and relatively intangible; and when asked to articulate it teachers find this difficult (like many good painters and musicians). None the less, it is an important factor in determining what goes on in schools and classrooms.

Philosophers like Carr (2003) suggest that part of the problem stems from a failure to make a clear distinction between education and schooling. Briefly, 'schooling' is a term for what goes on in schools. Some of this might be, and much of it clearly should be, 'educational' in aim. But schools also have other aims like socialisation, childcare, and development of the workforce for economic growth and purposes such as certification and selection for further training and occupational roles. 'Education' by contrast involves being introduced to activities with their own intrinsic value, in a morally acceptable way and with an emphasis on understanding and cultivating a broad intellectual perspective. Hence issues of, say, class management and discipline, or of educational aims and curriculum considerations turn on values and relationships based on principles like respect for persons, freedom, and equality. Many educational philosophers and sociologists see themselves as engaged in a constant struggle to direct teachers' and policy-makers' attention to these values and issues. Educational thinking, they argue, should not be reduced to the mechanical interpretation of standards, as if all that was involved was a simple set of technical teaching skills.

Some student teachers initially wonder about the need for extended theory in training courses, especially when so much is a matter of continuing debate. They think they would prefer clear guidance about what to do and be left to get on with learning how to do it. There is certainly a point to be made here since teachers are constrained by the need to act (to face Primary 5 or Form 4b on Monday morning) and can't forever debate different approaches and theories.

All teaching, however, inevitably reflects some kind of theory and as such invites critical scrutiny. Teaching is too important, complex and hotly debated to be reducible to a simple set of recipes and simplistic ideas about 'what works'. Moreover, student teachers are known already to have a strong sense of educational values when they begin training and the contested nature of these issues will not go away. They can't just be swept under the educational carpet. The forces at work inevitably affect teachers' room for manoeuvre in the classroom. Making effective practical professional decisions demands awareness of the issues at stake and of the operative factors. To fail to do so is to remain at the mercy of these forces, to the detriment of the quality of education you can provide for your learners. A complex blend of values, aims, ideas and practical judgement is what needs to inform educational decisions in the classroom. Moreover, it is this that makes the study and practice of education unendingly absorbing and challenging. It touches on so many aspects of life and society – its values, history, cultural issues, questions about the nature of knowledge and the interpretation and application of research findings. These issues and challenges are interwoven with the interactive challenges posed by teaching and managing children and young people, team-working with colleagues, learning to work in partnership with parents and so on. It will be useful to keep all this in mind in exploring the various topics in the chapters which follow.

PART I
Studying Education

2 TEACHING AND LEARNING

THE DEBATE ON TEACHING AND LEARNING

At school and in university we become aware that teachers have different styles and use different methods, and that some are patently much more effective than others. It is natural, however, to expect that after '3,000 years of educational wisdom' (the title of a classic American text) some consensus about teaching methods will have been achieved. Surely the combined insights of theoretical discussion, practical experience and the findings of research have produced clarity about what different kinds of teaching exist and what methods suit different subjects and classes. Surely, teacher education courses straightforwardly explain these findings and methods so that newly qualified teachers can proceed to apply them in the classroom. Certainly, research on teaching and learning has never been so intense, so closely connected to actual teaching in school and so practical in its implications as it is today. There is much that is agreed and there are many skills to learn which have been shown to improve classroom teaching. Yet there is also a very lively debate about teaching and learning and the issues are considerably more complex than they first appear.

In reading about different kinds of teaching you quickly come across what seems to be a complete ragbag of terms and ideas: traditional, progressive, child-centred, activity, whole-class lessons, group work, project work, discovery learning. You need to find explanations of these terms and a way of organising these ideas that makes sense. Soon further questions arise. Is teaching style the same as teaching method or strategy? How do matters of class organisation fit in? How many different kinds of teaching exist? What makes them different from one other? What has research to say about the matter? This chapter aims to answer these questions in a way that you will find helpful as you think about teaching on placement, read books and articles on teaching methods and write up assignments. It begins by looking at attempts to compare different approaches to teaching.

One influential research study by Neville Bennett (1976) set out to compare the effects of traditional and progressive (or child-centred) teaching approaches. By traditional he meant formal teaching with the children sitting in rows and much direct instruction by the teacher. In contrast, progressive methods were those where the atmosphere was more informal, pupils sat in groups and the emphasis was on learning through active tasks and projects where pupils conducted their own enquiries. They were child-centred in the sense that the teacher aimed to use children's interests as a starting point for planning learning activities, and helped them retain ownership of the direction of their learning and enquiry, albeit within some broad overall curriculum plan managed by the teacher. The researchers began by working with a spectrum of twelve different styles or strategies, ranging from very traditional to very progressive. In the end, the difficulty of making such fine distinctions among teaching approaches forced the researchers to reduce their categories to three groups – 'traditional', 'progressive' and 'mixed'. The results were hotly debated. They claimed to show that in language and mathematics pupils made better progress under traditional approaches. It became clear, however, that the dispute was as much about educational aims and values as about teaching methods. If your aim was a narrow drilling in the 'three Rs' then, not surprisingly, formal methods worked best. Progressive teachers had wider aims for curriculum and learning however, and their open, enquiry-based teaching had clear strengths for these purposes.

Since Bennett's investigation there have been other attempts to classify and compare teaching approaches. Each research project has tended to develop its own labels for different kinds of teaching. The ORACLE study (Galton 1999) identified six styles of classroom interaction with labels such as 'individual enquirers' and 'frequent changers'. This study demonstrated how much time in some styles teachers spend just managing and organising children as opposed to actually teaching them. Surprisingly, it found that it was in whole-class discussion, not small group teaching, that the most effective, open-ended questioning occurred. Once again, however, the researchers failed to develop convincing distinctions between styles (Barrow 1984) and their classification of teaching approaches never caught on.

In the research literature a large number of differently labelled teaching strategies can be found though many of these refer to particular tactics like questioning, probing and role-play rather than to broader strategies. Joyce et al. (2000) argue that the accomplished teacher should command a repertoire of seventeen different 'models of teaching'. These models are grouped into four main families, reflecting the particular psychological ideas (information processing, self-development, social learning, behaviourism) underlying the different groups. The complexity of this analysis is probably the main reason it has never found favour among other researchers or practising teachers.

Other approaches have had a similar fate, with the result that among theorists and researchers there is no agreed classification of teaching types, no consensus about what different kinds of teaching exist or what makes them different from one another. It is no surprise therefore, that many researchers, policy-makers and teachers have shied away from the question and focused instead on trying to identify the characteristics of good teaching in general. This approach has produced lists of attributes like being organised, a good communicator and so on (see, for example Muijs and Reynolds 2001). It also has its problems, however. Firstly, it is not clear that there are such general skills that can be learned in an educational vacuum and then applied to particular contexts. Secondly, any repertoire of skills needs to be brought into some sort of co-ordinated whole in any actual teaching context not just turned on one at a time. Thirdly, and most importantly, if one thing has become obvious over the years it is that there is no one best way to teach. Aims, contexts, subjects, stages of development differ and so teachers need different teaching approaches to take account of this. The teaching profession badly needs a simple, yet powerful and flexible, classification of teaching that is theoretically sound and practically useful.

There is in fact a classification of teaching that meets these criteria – the theory of teaching modes. Since there is no comprehensive exposition of this theory in a single source, perhaps it will be helpful here to outline its main features. This broad framework of ideas about teaching modes should help you make sense of the variety of teaching and the debate on teaching and learning, and enable you to make effective classroom decisions about teaching methods.

MODES OF TEACHING

The theory of teaching modes (see Skinner 1994) suggests that basically there are four quite distinct kinds, or modes, of teaching:

- direct teaching;
- enquiry;
- discussion;
- action learning.

It argues that the effective teacher has a mastery of each mode – a clear grasp of their differing requirements and the ability to deploy them in a skilful, balanced and flexible way.

You should think of a teaching mode as a form or structure of teaching. An analogy with the idea of forms or genres in the arts might help. In literature, for example, it has proved useful to distinguish the modes (some call them genres) of tragedy, comedy, romance and so on. In music there are different forms or structures such as fugue, sonata and rondo. The point is that, like modes in the arts, in teaching each of the four modes refers to a distinctive type of teaching. All teaching is not the same, nor is all music or literature: there are distinctly different forms and these operate in quite different ways.

The modes differ from one another in five main ways:

- the means of learning;
- organisation and resources;
- teacher and learner roles;
- teaching skills;
- typical assessment approaches.

Each of the four modes is considered below, using these five differentiating features, to get a feel for their distinctive aspects, what it means to teach using them and what issues emerge for further study and research.

Direct teaching

Means of learning
The means or basis of learning is through the direct presentation of ideas, information and skills, using instruction and demonstration. It might involve the teacher explaining ideas and concepts, presenting factual knowledge in an ordered form, outlining or demonstrating a skill, scientific procedure or effect.

Organisation and resources
The best organisation is in rows (it need not be serried ranks) or more informally facing the teacher – the presumed source of knowledge. Resources involve some presentation aids such as a whiteboard, overhead projector or laptop and specific visual aids or examples. Many scientific and environmental processes are now effectively demonstrated using computer-generated models.

Teacher and learner roles

The roles of teacher and learner are clear-cut: giver and receiver. This raises the question of what a learner needs to do to absorb information and ideas effectively from direct teaching. Is it not best done in an active, questioning way? And how can the teacher present material to make it easy for the learners to grasp the ideas?

Teaching skills

Direct instruction places a premium on classic teaching skills like explaining, demonstrating and structuring knowledge for learners. As a teacher you not only need to know your subject well but need to know how to present it in a way that enables learners to quickly understand. This means structuring your explanation effectively and being inventive about examples, images and analogies to suit your learners. For this you have to understand your learners, who will often be of mixed levels of experience.

Another important set of skills in direct teaching is motivating and keeping attention and classroom discipline. In most school classrooms these aspects need to be worked hard at. Motivating resources can be a great help here as can humour and force of personality. In infant classrooms the teacher has often to be a bit larger than life, to put on a performance. All this makes direct teaching a challenge.

Assessment

A great aid to direct teaching is knowing your learners and checking they are with you. In school situations this is where oral questioning plays such a vital role, questioning to check understanding as you proceed with your explanation or information giving. Following direct teaching, worksheets, practice problems and exercises to apply and test understanding are common.

Issues

The main issues for direct teaching are differentiation, keeping attention and motivation. Traditionally, questioning was thought to involve pupils actively and provide motivation but this has often proved far from successful. More recently there has been strong advocacy of whole-class interactive teaching. This is closely directed by the teacher who uses assertive questioning mixed with demonstration by pupils. Pupils have an active role and there is a co-operative ethos among the class. Chalk and talk, certainly, but the chalk is sometimes in a pupil's hands.

Research is beginning to indicate that many teachers who adopt whole-class interactive approaches are finding it difficult to move away from closed, low-level questioning, tight teacher control of interaction, and inadequate differentiation. ICT learning resources (like a computer-generated model of an active volcano, or the water cycle) can convey explanations and basic knowledge very effectively and their high presentation standards pose a strong challenge to traditional teacher explanations and demonstrations.

Enquiry

The enquiry mode has a double purpose: to teach subject understanding (for example, understanding of energy and forces) through enquiry; and to teach learners how to conduct an effective enquiry.

Means of learning
This is 'finding out for yourself,' through research, experiment, and investigation.

Organisation and resources
Enquiries can be by individuals or groups, structure and organisation varying with the discipline concerned, for example if it is history, science or art and design. In enquiry learning, resources (such as reference books, the Internet, apparatus, art materials and so on) are usually a prime consideration, and again vary with the research focus.

Teacher and learner roles

The teacher's role here is not instructor but adviser on the process of effective enquiry and resources, giving the learners ownership of the direction of enquiry while supporting and challenging them. To learn well in this mode, learners should be prepared to try relevant strategies, observe carefully, ask questions, experiment confidently and systematically and reflect critically on evidence.

Teaching skills

A central skill is to model effective enquiry for the learners. The teacher also needs to support and challenge learners, helping them to be disciplined but also open to ideas and evidence. At evaluation the teacher should be a constructive critic, encouraging pupils to ask questions and evaluate reflectively. These are very different skills from those of direct teaching.

Assessment

In genuine enquiry the outcomes are unpredictable, requiring a distinctive approach to assessment. Assessment often involves pupils reporting back orally, or in writing, on the results of investigations. Assessment typically covers observation and evaluation of process as well as consideration of outcome.

Issues

An important issue for enquiry learning is how far enquiry is discipline-specific as opposed to being based on a common enquiry process. The standard scientific enquiry process – observation, hypothesis, experiment – is not the basis for historical, literary or religious enquiry, though evidence is always a central concept and all such enquiries may culminate in analysis, evaluation, and reporting phases. This issue merges with the continuing debate on generic versus subject-specific thinking skills.

Another issue is the role of subject understanding. Can you learn to enquire in history, chemistry, literature without first knowing some basic history, chemistry or literature? If not, enquiry approaches need to be balanced by more structured learning using other modes, especially direct teaching.

Yet another issue concerns the degree of openness of the enquiry. You can think of a continuum from the learner's own open enquiry (of the properties of magnets, the behaviour of snails or exploration of working with clay) doubtless crossing subject boundaries, to more structured teacher-led projects on recycling waste or the Romans and to even more tightly structured problem-solving in mathematics or discovery learning in science. Open subject-crossing enquiry poses a curricular challenge given national curriculum prescriptions, and an organisational one with a whole class.

Discussion

It is useful to distinguish three main types of discussion:

- appreciative sharing of ideas/experiences;

- controversial issues;

- problem-solving/decision-making.

As with enquiry, teachers usually have a double aim: to develop knowledge and understanding through discussion; and to teach learners how to discuss effectively. The outcomes of effective discussion are usually deeper understanding, wiser judgement, greater awareness of significant factors, and better discussion skills.

Means of learning
Pupils learn through interaction, by reasoning and argument. Dillon (1994) identifies two main aspects to this. They enrich their understanding and they refine their understanding. Enrichment comes from the diversity of views participants express, and from the process of reflecting and responding. Refinement comes from being forced, as a participant, to be

clear about what you are saying, to support your views with evidence and to be consistent in what you say.

Organisation and resources

The aim is to promote interaction among all participants. You need a circle or semi-circle, not rows. Eye contact is crucial. In schools some concrete props or recent experience as the stimulus or focus for discussion is helpful, even for general issues like war or fox hunting.

Teacher and learner roles

The teacher's role is to model discussion skills and conduct the flow of conversation ensuring it proceeds according to basic values inherent in a good discussion – like equality, freedom, respect for persons, and truth (Bridges 1978). The learner's role is to participate, be a good listener, develop confidence in expressing a view, and argue reasonably.

Teaching skills

These include modelling appropriate participation in discussion and facilitating discussion without resort to question and answer.

Assessment

This is usually observation or recording of the process, particularly the quality of reasoning but also of aspects like listening, turn taking, and confidence in expressing views. Assessment of outcomes like deeper understanding is usually through later associated activities – written work, practical projects and also future discussions – since skill and understanding in discussing poems, novels or environmental issues build over time.

Issues

The main issue in teaching through discussion is the role of questioning. Teachers have traditionally been taught that questioning is the way to encourage pupil thinking, manage the flow of discussion and encourage participation. Extensive research and theory from Dillon (1988) has strongly questioned this approach. He advocates a strict avoidance of questioning in handling discussion and the use of alternatives (see Chapter 4). Teacher questions turn discussion into question and answer and usually fail to promote participation.

Action learning

This covers activity methods, experiential learning, role play and simulations.

Means of learning
The essence is learning by doing. The focus is on direct experience, learning how, not just learning that. However, this mode also recognises that the quality of learning through action depends heavily on the quality of thinking about action. But such thinking is not necessarily overt during the action. Besides, as Hamlet discovered, there can be a tension between thinking and acting. These need to be effectively balanced ensuring the action is properly planned for, sustained, and reflected. In action learning, the learning process is best seen as a cycle of planning, doing and reflecting.

Organisation and resources
This clearly depends on the activity. Learning to model with clay is different from learning to referee a game, practise the violin, conduct an experiment, organise a concert, participate in a citizenship or enterprise simulation.

Teacher and learner roles
The teacher's role is to involve learners fully in planning and reflecting, not just to direct or push them through the activity. Learners need to be encouraged to sustain the action. These are support and challenge roles. In some action learning there is a tradition of more directive coaching. The learner needs to own and participate effectively in all phases of the action learning cycle.

Teaching skills
These include providing encouragement and feedback without hindering effective action and learner-owned planning and reflection.

Assessment
Observation is obviously crucial, along with reflective pupil self-assessment. Structured feedback from the teacher can be important.

Issues
The main danger is pushing learners through the action and not involving them in the planning and reflecting phases and judging how structured or open the learning should be. Potentially fruitful and deep learning about measurement and applied mathematics would be largely lost if, say, the activity of making a Christmas cracker were planned only by the teacher and assessed only by the teacher with children merely following close production instructions.

Whatever the extent of structuring, the essence of action learning is always learning by doing and the issues are the role of thinking, ownership of learning, reflection and feedback. This makes it distinct from most direct teaching contexts. It should be said here that worksheets, seen through the lens of modes theory, are often not genuine action learning but fundamentally tests to assess knowledge gained through direct teaching with some pencil and paper application problems. There is a great deal more to action learning than a standard worksheet mentality acknowledges.

THE VALUE OF THE MODES THEORY

Some educationists argue that if we identify the common features of any good teaching and train teachers in these skills the quality of teaching and hence of pupil learning will greatly improve. There is some sense in this. Explaining, being enthusiastic, thinking about the learner, knowing the subject matter

well, finding interesting ways to motivate learners, structuring and linking to previous learning are critical features of
good teaching.

However, some difficulties with this common features
approach were noted earlier. Having now outlined each of the
four modes, a further criticism can be made. It badly under-
plays the differences between the various types of teaching.
The theory of teaching modes does not deny the similarities
but it focuses on the differences since these are at least as
crucial to effective teaching as supposedly general qualities.
Teachers need to understand that there are fundamentally different ways of approaching teaching and to realise, while
acknowledging certain common characteristics, just how different teaching roles, organisation, and so on are from mode
to mode. They also need to learn to switch as the situation
demands from one mode to another.

The theory is simple, yet powerful, balanced and open. It is
admirably simple in the sense that we have to come to terms
with only four modes not seventeen models or eighty different strategies. A busy teacher could work with four modes;
seventeen different models are impracticable. It is powerful in
that it gets to the heart of the decisions teachers need to make
– about aims, teaching and learning roles, assessment and so
on. Aspects that at first seem unrelated are quickly brought
into a single perspective; for example assessment strategies
can be quickly checked to see they are consistent with other
features of that particular mode. It is clearly a balanced
theory. It does not say there is one best way to teach, nor does
it try to arbitrate between traditional direct teaching and progressive open enquiry. It says both have a clear place. The
good teacher needs to deploy all four modes in a balanced way
to meet the range of contexts, subjects (and their different
aspects) and aims. It moves beyond the sterile debate between
traditional and progressive teaching. It is also an open theory,
able to be developed in response to further thinking and
research. Some think that because at the borderline it is difficult to distinguish, say, question and answer (in direct teaching) from discussion (a different mode) the theory falls down.

But consider areas such as drama where a Shakespeare play, like *The Winter's Tale*, has elements of tragedy and comedy (and indeed romance and pastoral) without making the idea of dramatic modes redundant. The modes are very helpful in understanding plays, perhaps particularly where plays are a mix of several modes. Drama, like teaching, is complex.

The same point could be made about musical forms. To appreciate Mozart's *Jupiter* symphony it helps to understand the interplay of fugue and about sonata form. Mozart certainly needed to understand them to decide what would best serve his intentions with the *Jupiter*. As with the arts, many of the interesting educational questions arise by working at such boundaries between modes. Working with the powerful concepts in many disciplines is like this. They are not all tightly defined as in mathematics. In education, the arts and social sciences ideas are more open, contested and problematic than we may at first assume or are initially comfortable with. Learning to think about teaching and education precisely involves coming to terms with this complexity, while using these powerful but problematic ideas to help make sense of teaching. Stenhouse (1975) noted that historians and students of history use concepts like cause and revolution to understand, say, the origins of the First World War and the French or agrarian revolutions and, in doing so, they come to understand the concepts and their complexities more deeply.

Teaching mode is not yet a commonly used term outside of Scotland but it does relate to ideas which can be found clearly in a range of books and articles on enquiry methods, action learning and teaching through discussion (for example Dillon 1988; Pring 1976; Boud et al. 1993). There are two other features of the modes theory which make it worthy of attention. First, it is valid at the level of common sense. According to Powell (1985) there are, at root, four basic ways of learning something:

- having something explained directly;
- by reason and argument;

- by direct experience;
- finding out for ourselves.

These are, you will recognise, just the four modes of teaching. Secondly, it has deep roots in the history of education and in the standard range of teaching approaches in higher education:

- lectures (direct teaching);
- seminars (meant to be discussions, though too often they become mini-lectures);
- practicals (action learning);
- projects/dissertations (enquiry).

Three further points of clarification may help. First, it is of course probable that in a given lesson more than one mode can often be used – for example, direct teaching followed by enquiry or discussion. However, if within a lesson a teacher is constantly switching modes then there is a danger of falling between two or more stools and doing nothing effectively. Each mode requires different roles, organisation and resourcing and it is better to give each mode a sustained period to enable it to do its work. Deciding what is a good balance in using the different modes can't, however, be a simple matter of devoting equal time to each mode. A more sophisticated professional judgement, taking account of the particular teaching context and aims is required.

Secondly, 'teaching mode' is also different from 'class organisation' (whole class, group, individual). It is much more than a means of grouping learners. The differences between modes centre on different means of learning and therefore differing teacher and learner roles. Class organisation is only one part of teaching mode, not the only or necessary distinguishing feature. Unfortunately some attempts to classify teaching have focused mainly on class organisation which is not at the core of teaching differences. So far as class organisation is concerned the longstanding official policy in Scotland is hard to beat. It is that there should be a 'judicious and flexible blend of whole class, group and individual instruction.'

Finally, in education the temptation to seek 'the one best way' as a panacea for the ills of teaching remains strong and candidates like whole-class interactive teaching, accelerated or brain-based learning, and constructivist teaching capture the profession's collective imagination. Such approaches always turn out to be only partial answers. Nor can a single approach suit a particular school subject. Since national curricula have a wide range of aims and teaching and learning are complex phenomena, it is unlikely there is one best way to teach to realise them. Teaching needs to be seen as an area for careful research and development within a wide and realistic framework. The sad fact is that it has proved very difficult for schools or teaching at any level to move far away from direct teaching approaches and traditional assumptions about roles and procedures. This may relate closely to concerns over teacher control of learning, reinforced by pressures from national curriculum targets.

The modes theory can be practically useful and theoretically illuminating. Suddenly everything comes into perspective and makes sense. You see the difference between question and answer which is basically an adjunct to direct teaching to test knowledge and check understanding, and the very different aims and methods of a genuine discussion which is geared to exploring issues that are truly open to discussion. Likewise, ideas emerge about the role of questioning in the various modes (see Chapter 4). This makes a big difference to classroom practice and pupil learning and teacher satisfaction. Teaching involves a wide range of skills and qualities. Understanding the four modes theory and using the modes in a balanced way enables you to deploy these skills to full effect for the benefit of pupil learning. An excellent personal target in a training course would be to understand and be able to use confidently each mode in relation to your specialist or favourite subject.

3 CURRICULUM AND ASSESSMENT

It goes without saying that to be a good teacher you need to know the subject matter you are teaching thoroughly and be skilled at finding out how well your pupils have learned what you have taught. But there is more to the school curriculum than knowing subject content. Likewise, assessing pupil learning isn't just a matter of giving regular tests and preparing pupils for exams. To qualify as a teacher you need a wider and deeper grasp of these two important, and closely related, areas of curriculum and assessment. This chapter aims to help you make sense of them. The first part focuses on curriculum, the second on assessment.

WHAT IS CURRICULUM?

Curriculum used to be thought of as more or less a syllabus – a list of subjects to be taught and specific content to be mastered. Nowadays it tends to be given a very broad definition. Some educationists think of curriculum as all the learning, planned and unplanned, that takes place in a school. This makes a point but is probably too wide to be otherwise useful. Important distinctions have been made (McCormick and Murphy 2000) between the prescribed curriculum (for example, what is laid down in national guidelines), the enacted curriculum (what the teacher actually provides in class) and the experienced curriculum (what the pupils actually experience as groups or individuals). Research has shown that there can be big gaps between all three.

Another important idea is that of the hidden curriculum – the unconscious messages learners receive from educational contexts and experiences about values and priorities. Schools need to be especially vigilant that curricula and educational institutions don't in fact subtly teach discrimination or build in inequitable treatment for various groups. This means being alert to ideological messages and particular values that the curriculum content and organisation may be conveying.

An important question is who decides (or should decide) the curriculum? The answer has differed with time and place. The official curriculum represents a set of compromises among various stakeholders and reflects the history, politics, economics and culture of a country. In some countries, parents have a strong say; in others, central government or academic experts; in others, local groups; and in yet others, teachers have more actual influence. Debate surrounds who has a legitimate right to have a say and who is in the best position to make good decisions about what pupils should learn.

Curriculum philosophers have been influential in urging a basic framework centred on a supposed core of distinct, fundamental forms of knowledge (Kelly 2004) but it is useful to remember here the distinction between education and schooling referred to in Chapter 1. The curriculum needs to reflect a defensible view of the nature of knowledge but other considerations (for example, social and economic ones) need to inform decisions about its content. The actual enacted curriculum depends very much on teachers' understanding of policies and principles, while the received curriculum depends not only on pupils' responses but on the teacher's skills in explaining and motivating.

NATIONAL CURRICULA

Among the aims of introducing national curriculum specifications in the UK were those of securing an adequate educational entitlement for all pupils, improving continuity and progression in learning and higher standards, and providing better communication with, and information for, parents. Linked to the introduction of national testing, league tables,

and increasing choice and competition among schools, this
was expected to drive up standards.

These national curriculum developments have been subject
to numerous critiques over the years. What is now clear is that
national curricula are moving into a more open and creative
phase (see DfES 2003; Scottish Executive 2004) although
critics continue to point out that central control remains
strong as do the impacts of national testing, examinations and
top-down initiatives. But the new policy documents do signal
a move to greater curriculum flexibility, creativity and development of more coherent teaching around integrated curricular projects, along with allegedly generic aspects like
thinking and critical skills. This, briefly, is the background
against which discussion can now turn to the primary and secondary curriculum.

The primary curriculum

At first sight the curriculum knowledge needed for primary
teaching, as laid down in the standards, can look formidable,
a real challenge. How can you know everything about a dozen
different subjects for children aged three to twelve? Primary
teachers handle this successfully day in and day out, however,
and they started on the same basis as you. While there are high
expectations about teachers' knowledge of the curriculum,
there is also now a wide range of very helpful ideas and
resources for teaching. It is clearly not realistic to expect
primary teachers to display specialist expertise over the full
range of subjects. What you do need is a sound grasp of the
aims and nature of these subjects and their role in the primary
school; a basic grasp of their key concepts, facts and skills; and
ideas about how best to help children get inside these subjects.

Not every teacher will be passionate about every subject.
Each will have some preferences and subject strengths and
weaknesses. However, it is the wide range of subjects that
attracts many to primary teaching and many non-specialists
regularly teach drama, music, science and history well in

primary schools. Certainly, there is always more to learn, and becoming a consultant on a specialism in your school is a well-known career route in England. Team working provides additional levels of support in particular subjects such as science, and the trend is towards increasing specialist teaching at the upper primary stage across the UK. In Scotland, there are plans to increase the movement of teachers across the divide between upper primary and lower secondary.

Your course will help you develop these basic ideas and understandings and offer a wealth of practical ideas for teaching, even on a one-year programme, which you can store away until opportunities arise. This will build confidence and encourage you to find and develop other such ideas for yourself using resource networks (see Useful websites). You will be introduced to the rationale for the subject, its role in primary teaching, typical pupil misconceptions, the stages through which children progress in the subject, and the content, learning outcomes, targets and programmes of study children are expected to follow.

The secondary curriculum

Secondary teachers, it might be thought, need only be concerned with their subject. The curriculum is laid down by the government, they already have expert subject knowledge from university and surely the task is now to learn to teach their subject well, within the time allotted to it. This approach will no longer do, however. As is discussed in Chapter 8, teachers have a wider role than just subject teaching. They need to play a part in furthering the broad aims and cross-curricular teaching of the school. It is not a matter of subject teaching in a vacuum but of developing an understanding of the modern rationale of the secondary curriculum, its structures, overall aims, the balance between academic and vocational learning, and how all this relates to teaching particular subjects. Moreover, as Chapter 8 makes clear, the national curriculum has turned out to be not something fixed but rather something

constantly developing, and subject to changing ideas, priorities and, increasingly, interaction across subjects.

Two generic issues are being given increased attention. One
is literacy across the curriculum, as the way in which literacy
interacts with subject understanding and the ability to access
learning in any area has become clearer. All subjects are now
viewed as having a responsibility to develop appropriate literacy and there is a clear case for co-ordination across depart-
ments. Critical thinking (also called thinking skills) is another
area where all subjects have a role and which many claim has
important generic aspects. The generic nature of critical and
thinking skills is a continuing matter of dispute, however.
Some theorists argue strongly for the subject-specific nature
of these abilities (for example, Johnson 2001).

Concerns about the extent of disaffection from school (with
consequent early leaving) are leading secondary subject teachers to develop approaches to their subjects that pupils will find
more motivating and meaningful. Primary-secondary links
are important here along with larger, cross-curricular projects
involving co-operation among subject teachers, while also
ensuring solid development of individual subject understanding. This is clearly a major challenge. Personal, social and
health education, citizenship and developing an appropriate
balance between academic and vocational approaches in the
secondary school are other features that are widening the role
of secondary teachers away from traditional academic subject
teaching.

New secondary teachers will need to keep abreast of the
policy debate and developments occurring in schools. New
frameworks are being developed to help all reach their potential, with government targets such as aiming for 50 per cent of
the age group to enter higher education as compared to 10 per
cent in 1960. Other features are more choice to meet the needs
of learners, more flexibility about progression through the
school curriculum, more individualisation of learning paths
and increased links with work-based learning. Teachers are
now expected to be familiar with such curricular developments,
to plan accordingly and to give full weight to the role of ICT.

SUBJECT KNOWLEDGE AND TEACHING

Governments everywhere show concern to improve teachers' subject knowledge and understanding, whether it is primary teachers' grasp of science, their knowledge about language, or the updating of secondary teachers' knowledge of their disciplines. The relationship between subject knowledge and teaching approaches is complex, however. Along with good subject understanding at their own level, primary and secondary teachers need to know how to structure and present curriculum knowledge for learners – the best examples, analogies and ways of motivating pupils to learn the subject ('pedagogical content knowledge' in the clumsy curriculum jargon). Some graduates have excellent subject knowledge but can't put it across well. That is a different skill or achievement and needs to be learned.

The answer to the question 'What is a subject?' seems obvious – until you start to think carefully. For example is mathematics a body of knowledge – a set of clearly defined facts, concepts and skills which pupils have to master? Or is it best conceived as an activity – a problem-solving activity and means of communicating supported by this body of knowledge? Should pupils be taught the knowledge and skills first, then how to solve problems; should they develop understanding and skills through the experience of addressing various mathematical problems; or should both approaches interact? Is a concrete approach to teaching better than an abstract one and how does this depend on the age of the learner? Writings on mathematics education continue to debate these issues (Morgan et al. 2004). Other subjects – history, religious education, English, and so on – pose equally formidable, although different, problems.

Motivation is not just a matter of psychology. There are questions about showing pupils the intrinsic interest and worth of a discipline and of commitment to it, as opposed to dressing up its surface features to make it palatable. A balance needs to be struck here. Pupils need time to grasp the intrinsic interest and worth of many secondary subjects, especially in a heavily exam-oriented approach. At the same time, they need to be enthused quickly by being shown its relevance to their present lives, while also reinforcing the point that to learn something worthwhile and satisfying normally involves considerable work and determination.

Recent studies have shown that teachers have their own mental pictures of their subject. This is usually an amalgam of past knowledge, experience of learning it, and a personal view of what counts as good teaching, and of the purpose of the subject. All teachers can expect to develop their view of their subject throughout their career. Subjects are not static nor entities with laid-down answers, as a brief glance at the range of approaches to, for example English, economics or politics at universities across the land would quickly demonstrate. There is also the school reality of the subject – the book, texts, curriculum examples and procedures that constitute learning the subject in school. As a teacher you will find it helpful to work around these three conceptions – the university discipline, your own construct or perspective, and the school reality of the discipline as experienced and taught through the curriculum (Banks et al. 1999).

CURRICULUM PRINCIPLES

Curriculum principles are usually listed as breadth, balance, coherence, continuity and progression. Many now add depth, and give this a high priority. These principles are presented in official curriculum documents as ones which readily command the assent of teachers and educators. And guidelines expect that these principles will inform teachers' plans and practice. They appear to provide criteria against which to consider curriculum plans. Is this scheme of work a coherent one? Does it have good breadth and balance? Is there a clear progression in learning?

There is a sense in which this is perfectly sound. Who would be able to defend an incoherent curriculum or one where students made no or very little progress in learning? Persistent evidence of poor progression as pupils moved from primary to secondary education was one motivation for introducing the National Curriculum in England and Wales and why the 5–14 programme in Scotland took upper primary and lower secondary stages into one overall curriculum scheme. These principles need close and critical scrutiny, however, and they turn out to be labels for issues and problems, not practical prescriptions of how to act in planning your curriculum (Carr 2003). They don't tell you what conception of balance is appropriate (a balanced diet, a physical balance, a judicial one?) nor how to decide what is the best balance between different subjects. They merely indicate that balance is one important consideration.

Governments around the world have rarely hesitated to lay down expected percentages of time to be devoted to different curriculum areas. However, these decisions are usually political compromises among the stakeholders about what should have priority. Any agreed balance tends to be quickly overturned in practice as new priorities emerge in the official educational consciousness. For example, citizenship, physical education and enterprise education are now expected to feature strongly alongside the continuing high priority of language and mathematics.

THE PROCESS CURRICULUM

Some educators argue that we should think of the curriculum, not as content or outcomes but as a process of learning. For example, in science education this means emphasising the 'process'(in truth the activity, thinking and skills) of being a scientist, such as conducting fair experiments, learning how to observe and record carefully and how to develop explanations of cause and effect. There is less emphasis on memorising the content and findings of particular scientific topics, such as magnetism or the periodic table. Subject content will often be outdated by the time pupils leave school and some therefore think it is more important to learn methods and principles. In arts education, it is common to hear teachers assert that 'the process is more important than the product'. In areas of knowledge, however, you just can't separate process and product in a simple way. A good process is surely bound to lead to a good product. Can you imagine a bad drawing resulting from a good drawing process? Of course, at certain stages of learning there may be virtue in focusing on one aspect, and the traditional concern to pronounce on children's painting or musical efforts and to assume only a few have (apparently inborn) talents worth developing needs to be strongly resisted.

'Processes' can't be effectively developed without some conceptual understanding and basic factual knowledge. Learners need to know some history, religion, chemistry and whatever if they are to experiment intelligently, work productively with art resources, and so on. How else will they grasp the concept of time in history, learn not just techniques of painting but their point and purpose, or be able to apply scientific ideas to their everyday lives? Stenhouse's idea of a 'process curriculum' based on open enquiry learning and guided by principles of procedure instead of pre-specified content and objectives (Stenhouse 1975) certainly has some virtue in terms of enquiry learning. But other writings (for example, Kelly 2004) which view the process curriculum as involving a developmental process from inside the learner with specific learning determined by their inner needs tend to prove rather slippery. Besides, it gives insufficient recognition to the role of direct, structured teaching and to the fact that you cannot easily separate process and product. Learning is not well conceived as a matter of some internal psychological process but of induction into publicly available and justified knowledge (Carr 2003).

ASSESSMENT

One educationist asserted, with some justice, that if you want to know the truth about an educational system you should look at its assessment procedures. Assessment has a very important influence on teaching and learning and also on the curriculum that learners actually receive, whatever the rhetoric in curriculum plans and national guidance. Another reason for paying close attention to this topic is that assessment is the aspect of teacher training that often seems to be least well done, the one for which, ironically, students tend to get the lowest grades. Traditional assessment is probably the most technical aspect of teaching and conceptually among the most difficult. As usual in such circumstances, developing a good grasp of basic ideas is essential, for then everything becomes manageable and professionally interesting. This is what the discussion below aims to help you achieve.

Teacher education standards typically lay down a wide range of concepts, techniques and professional procedures that new teachers should be familiar with, such as reliability and validity, criterion and norm-referencing, baseline, formative and summative assessment. The assessment scene, however, has changed significantly in the last few years with school systems around the world beginning to show a softening of national testing regimes and a new emphasis on formative assessment. However, alongside this, many old assumptions and practices continue. You need to see the total picture.

To assess means to judge the worth, value or importance of something and in an educational context it usually means judging what has been learned or what learners are able to do. The key point is this idea of evidence of learning or ability. Bear that in mind whenever you think about assessment and you will find that writings on assessment begin to make sense and that you can make good decisions about assessment methods in the classroom. There are different ways in which you can gather evidence about learning. Teachers can look for evidence in what pupils do, write or say, by observing them at work and by examining the things they produce.

Teachers are usually urged to provide a balance of assessment methods linked to the nature of what is being learned. It is not a matter of variety for its own sake but because some learners are able to demonstrate their knowledge more effectively in one way than in another, and because the kind of evidence appropriate to a particular learning outcome might be more easily found using a particular method. For example, 'reporting back' exposes children's misconceptions and knowledge in a way that close teacher questioning will not. Questioning will freeze some pupils without necessarily exposing their thinking. One of the difficulties teachers face is that measuring learning or intellectual abilities is not a simple matter like measuring someone's height or weight. For a start, there are quite different kinds of things to learn – facts, concepts, skills, attitudes, procedures, performances – and they require different kinds of assessment. Complex learning like writing an imaginative story or conducting a mathematical or historical investigation can't be reduced to a bundle of simple, isolated skills which can be separately measured and assumed to add up to the whole performance or intellectual achievement.

Your thinking about assessment will be greatly helped if you understand the difference between a measurement model and a standards model of assessment (Biggs 2003). The idea behind a measurement model is to measure a particular ability on a scale so that individuals can be compared. Think of measuring height or weight. Traditional tests and exams are based on this kind of thinking. Measurement models are good for research and for ascertaining how well a student is doing compared with other students – for example how well someone's reading compares with others of the same age. However, such an approach to assessment has been shown to have a bad backwash effect on teaching and learning, demotivating those who do badly and often convincing them that they lack ability. In contrast, a standards model is very suitable for assessing learning and teaching. It looks at the quality of learning rather than the quantity and has much more positive effects on learning if used formatively as well as summatively (to sum up and record what has been achieved) and for planning future learning. This is something quite new for many educational contexts which have hitherto paid only lip service to formative assessment.

Formative assessment

Formative assessment is now widely championed as a key to educational transformation. It has come very much to the fore on the basis of impressive research studies and nationwide development work in schools (Thomas and Pring 2004). Some indication of the change in traditional practices it is beginning to induce in schools can be obtained by considering slogans now to be found in materials for teachers: 'pupils learn more by feedback than instruction', 'formative assessment significantly raises attainment', 'the less work the teacher does the better'.

So what is formative assessment and how does it operate? You need first to be aware of the basic difference between formative and summative assessment. Formative assessment is assessment where the main aim is to improve learning. This is done by assessing during the course of learning and offering diagnosis and feedback. By contrast, the aim of summative assessment is to sum up the extent and quality of learning. It is usually carried out by a test at the end of a unit of learning or end of a course. The important point to note, however, is that the difference is not essentially one of method or timing but of aim. You could use an end of term course exam assessment for formative purposes – to improve learning in the next term – if you gave detailed feedback on where students went wrong, their strengths and weaknesses, in good time for them to take advantage of it.

The development of formative assessment promises to have a number of important effects on traditional classroom interaction. One is the new emphasis on sharing learning outcomes with pupils. Hitherto this was not thought important nor was it well done. In a formative assessment context, however, it is vital. It requires skill to explain the intended learning in a way that pupils can understand. As a teacher you need to translate national curriculum targets and expected outcomes into goals for specific lessons and communicate them in language that makes sense to your learners. Some teachers are now discovering the value of involving pupils in articulating learning outcomes for a set of lessons or small project. This helps pupils become aware of criteria for success in learning.

There has been an equally big change in the role and practice of questioning. Formative assessment requires asking more challenging, open-ended questions. This is necessary to check understanding of complex learning and simple closed questions are inadequate for this. Clear learning outcomes are half the battle in many forms of teaching, but some complex learning needs to be open-ended for effective learning to occur. Among the new strategies of questioning are carefully planning questions; providing more wait time after asking (three to five seconds); asking more open-ended questions which explore thinking; and encouraging pupils to explore answers together. One development may come as a surprise, namely, abandoning asking for hands up. It is no longer a race to see who knows the correct answer but rather the aim is to generate a supportive climate where teacher and pupils are comfortable with wrong answers, and with 'I don't know'. Pupils now work together for the thoughtful improvement of answers instead of assuming it has to be right first time.

There are other changes, too. Rich follow-up activities are beginning to replace routine worksheets. Self and peer assessment are given a big role and pupils need to be trained carefully for this. 'Traffic light' signalling by pupils to indicate if they have good, partial, or little understanding, to which the teacher then responds with differentiated support, is very popular. Marks, it has become clear through research, are not particularly helpful to learning and may have a negative effect on pupils. It is the nature of feedback, not really the amount that is critical. The role of feedback is to help pupils learn better not to show how smart they are. Pupils benefit from rapid and regular feedback but providing constructive feedback is a skill. Advocates of formative assessment claim that, where it is given a full role, outcomes are deeper and there are long-lasting effects on pupils' self-awareness, confidence as learners and readiness to take control of their own learning, instead of remaining dependent on the teacher for advice on how to improve.

Taking this approach seriously at secondary level means defining the curriculum more broadly than just in terms of what will be tested, and having less frequent class tests, fewer examples of how to answer specific questions, and less feedback using grades, comparisons and competition for marks (Assessment Reform Group 2002). As a teacher it is important to gain trust from pupils because assessment can be a threatening process. Many freeze when questioned probingly. Remember, assessment is a social process, involving power relationships and is easily susceptible to inequities and biases. Assessment can have a deep (positive or negative) influence on motivation and self-esteem (Filer and Pollard 2000).

Most discussions of assessment assume a direct teaching context and this may be one reason why it has proved difficult to change teaching. Try thinking about assessment in relation to each of the different teaching modes discussed in Chapter 2.

Examinations, testing and performance data

Especially in secondary schools, although also in primary, there is now a wide range of data available on pupil and school performance. Many school managements and experienced teachers are learning to analyse such data, using computer software, and to adjust curriculum and teaching accordingly. As a new teacher you should be aware of these developments and be prepared to consider such evidence critically, along with other sources, in reviewing your teaching aims and methods. In doing so, it is crucial to bear in mind the dangers of using deficit model thinking (see Chapter 5) to quickly blame the pupils rather than looking closely at the curriculum and how it is taught.

It can be seen from the discussion in this chapter that assessment is a wide-ranging and rapidly developing aspect of teaching. It is very important to establish a firm foundation in this area because it has such a strong effect on other aspects of teaching. It is also important that assessment is properly balanced with teaching. A colleague used to put it well in his lectures, adapting a quote from Abraham Lincoln: 'Remember, you can assess some of the pupils some of the time, but you can't assess all of the pupils all of the time.'

4 DEVELOPMENTAL PSYCHOLOGY

To teach primary or secondary pupils well you need to recognise that they are rapidly developing as persons and remain alert to the fact that they have an active life beyond the classroom. Children and adolescents are learning a great deal outside school as well as in. Moreover, what is going on in their lives outside school can have a big effect on their behaviour and functioning in school. Developmental psychology can help you acquire a broad picture of the patterns of children's growth and development and help you understand the various influences on their lives and on the attitudes and abilities they display in class. Of course, teachers and schools cannot be expected to resolve all the problems arising from the out-of-school context in which children are growing up. They can, however, be sensitive to all these factors and to the individual as a whole person. They can also try to ensure that the class environment and school ethos is a positive and encouraging one, helping pupils to succeed in their studies and further their personal and social development.

Another important insight from psychological studies is just how much pupils' behaviour in the classroom depends on the teacher's own behaviour – on how the teacher interacts with his or her pupils. To take a simple example, it has been shown that a teacher (or parent) responding to a child's work with negative criticism only will de-motivate the child. Indiscriminate praise, however, will not in the end have much effect. But positive, specific praise offered in an open and non-patronising way will give the child confidence to try new things, not being afraid to make mistakes, and to improve performance. This may seem common sense yet the fact is that the first two are by far the most typical responses to children by parents (even well-educated ones) and teachers (even experienced ones). Research like this has uncovered many fruitful strategies teachers can use in interaction with children and demonstrated that problems might not only lie with the child.

Psychological studies have also cast light on how children acquire concepts and skills across the range of curriculum subjects, misconceptions they may develop, difficulties in learning they may experience, effects on self-esteem and the role of social factors in learning. As a result of all these potential contributions, developmental psychology has long had a firm place in teacher training and is usually very well received by students, some of whom become very interested. In a developmental psychology module for intending primary teachers the focus is likely to be on child development up to eleven or twelve, while for secondary teachers the main focus will be on the psychology of adolescence. However, both groups will benefit from understanding central features of primary and secondary age developments. Moreover, ideas like stage of development, scaffolding, and self-esteem are relevant to intending teachers at any level, as are basic theories of learning, intelligence and motivation. No one expects classroom teachers to be expert psychologists. Yet you need a good grasp of what psychology has to offer and an ability to apply ideas critically, and with good judgement, to school contexts. You need to learn to observe children carefully in the light of a general awareness of developmental patterns and issues, and theories of learning.

In building such a perspective, it is worth bearing in mind some facts about psychology as a field of study. Developmental psychology is a branch of a broader academic discipline – psychology as a whole. Specific studies of learning and children's development are influenced by debates within psychology generally, about methods of research and appropriate assumptions underlying studies of human thinking and behaviour. Psychology, like other contributory disciplines to education, is a rapidly developing area of research studies, not a static body of established knowledge. As a discipline it has had an eventful history, dominated at some times by one set of assumptions and research methods and at others by very different ideas and approaches. At the present time, several different schools of thinking co-exist and inform a range of theoretical and research studies. Psychology has had an important influence on education at the level of general ideas, frameworks and principles, and as a way of introducing teachers to children's perspectives on the world, their concerns, interests and motivations and how they relate to their peers.

Another factor to be aware of is that many of the issues researched and discussed by psychologists are also considered by philosophers and sociologists to be very much in their patch. For example, sociologists have painted a rather different picture of childhood from the one which has emerged from psychology, suggesting that development is generally much less individually determined (for example, Austin et al. 2003; Mayall 2003). Likewise, philosophers have been severely critical of one psychological school, behaviourism, as a theory of human learning, of key aspects of Piaget's theory of stages (as now have many psychologists) and have criticised some fashionable writings on ideas like self-esteem and emotional intelligence. To be sure, trainee teachers cannot be expected to arbitrate between disciplines, but it would be equally misguided to assume these differences don't exist and just ask for simple facts and implications for teaching. It is difficult for some to accept that there are no easy answers and yet the contributions of the various perspectives are important. Life in classrooms is complex and it is this that makes it interesting and gives teachers an important and challenging role.

How in a short course or even a long one can you make sense of all this for teaching? There is a danger of being overwhelmed with detail on, say, infant development and the critiques of Piaget's experiments, or of becoming generally cynical since development is an area of controversy and theories continue to change. The best approach, surely, is to be committed to understanding the learners you are teaching and to fostering their development as learners and persons. This implies becoming clear about the main ideas, accepted current findings and debates, and learning to look critically at evidence, arguments and ideas and thinking through the implications for teaching. By combining these insights from psychology with other ideas you can gradually develop a professional perspective on teaching. The alternative is to be unconsciously tied to yesterday's theories, (which is to what 'common sense' often boils down) which may be even less secure. One cannot escape psychological theory even if it is an outdated psychology rather than thinking based on new evidence and conceptualisation.

THE STAGES OF DEVELOPMENT CONTROVERSY

Piaget's idea of stages of development has dominated developmental psychology for many years and has had a major impact on curriculum and teaching. Although some of its central features have now been widely critiqued, it remains strongly influential in many respects. The basic idea is that children at different stages think in different ways. These are qualitatively different ways, not just quantitative differences. In Piaget's theory it is not just that children at a more advanced stage know more, are quicker, more fluent, or more secure (though this does seem to be the evidence emerging from information-processing studies of how children develop). The basis of their reasoning, Piaget suggested, is different at different stages. Briefly, Piaget identified four main stages of cognitive development: sensori-motor, pre-operational, concrete operations and formal operations. These terms are not readily obvious labels and require some explanation.

Sensori-motor: This Piagetian stage (0–2 years) is one at which thinking relies on a child's movements and reactions to stimuli in its environment. Activity is important for development.

Pre-operational: At this stage (2–6 years) children can use symbolic play and language to aid thinking. It is still dominated by perception; children find it difficult to see others' viewpoints, and they have not yet mastered conservation.

Concrete operations: At this stage (7–11 years) children can solve problems using concrete objects, for instance counting with coloured cubes, and can think about two attributes (like height and weight) simultaneously. They can now decentre, and show conservation and reversibility.

Formal operations: This stage (11 years onwards) features abstract adult thinking. Individuals can consider all possibilities, think ahead, hypothesise and solve problems using abstract symbols as well as concrete objects.

One main implication of this theory for teaching is that we need to match teaching to children's current attainments, to find out where children are developmentally and provide appropriate activities for them to work through the course of development at that stage. The implication is that the teacher should not try to push the child further forward but await the readiness for the next stage that will eventually come from maturation and appropriate stage-related development activities.

Research following Piaget's seminal work has made it clear that, while children develop in the sequences Piaget indicated, there is a considerable variation in the ages at which they reach each stage. Direct teaching appears to enable children to progress faster than if left to their own devices. Difficulties have been raised with Piaget's conception of readiness and critics have also questioned his interpretation of children's responses to his tests of conservation and all this in turn has led to questioning of his assertion that the stages represent qualitatively different kinds of thinking. Some prefer a theory of overlapping phases rather than strictly separate stages and point out that children can show considerable variation in what they can accomplish within each of Piaget's stages. There has also been much more attention recently to the social and linguistic aspects of learning and the role of peers and teachers in children's cognitive development than Piaget acknowledged.

B. F. SKINNER'S LEARNING THEORY

B. F. Skinner (1968) argued that people learn best by being rewarded rather than punished. Consequently, instead of punishing and constantly reprimanding wrong behaviour, a teacher should reward pupils whenever they do behave correctly or do things that could lead to better behaviour. Then, the theory goes, and research evidence confirms, they are more likely to act like this again and so a teacher can gradually shape the behaviour of a class or individual. You try to catch them being good, doing what you want. Rewarding such behaviour is what is known as positive reinforcement. For example, if misbehaving children are given a tangible reward when they show desirable behaviour, the evidence is that they are likely to continue acting like that. (In primary school rewards could be stars, sweets, play opportunities in 'golden time'; in secondary it is usually more adult choice options such as 'chat time' and involvement in a range of attractive events.) This basic idea has had a strong influence on class management policies, on pastoral and behavioural aspects of learning and on handling pupils with special needs and learning difficulties.

Skinner has been criticised as offering blind conditioning instead of character development and a reliance on extrinsic rather than intrinsic rewards. Critics argue that teachers should help pupils to appreciate the rewards inherent in moulding clay, the fascination of number patterns in the tables, or geometric patterns in tessellations, and the challenge of uncovering these, the pleasure of solving a difficult problem or carving out a poem through the hard work of drafting and redrafting. Behaviourists reply that extrinsic rewards are a route to appreciating the intrinsic rewards of learning. At least the class pays attention and there is some hope of getting them interested in algebra or whatever, whereas, otherwise, in many classrooms there would be little learning or enjoyment of it. Skinnerians claim that the method helps develop self-discipline and works in the short term.

In a wider perspective, and for the long term, however, a behaviourist approach is clearly inadequate. Education is surely fundamentally about the development of the mind and awareness of actions and responsibilities for them. While Skinner's ideas do have their roots in strong experimental research, the problem is that educational policies and judgements need to be based on aims and values and a proper conception of learning a subject. There has been some influential work on class management from this perspective (see Chapter 6) but again mere control can only be a partial perspective and aim.

SELF-ESTEEM

Two important ideas are self-concept and self-esteem though again some caveats are required. The development of identity involves a mix of personal traits, roles and relationships, background interests, values, beliefs, attitudes. Not all of these are necessarily stable. Self-concept is how persons see themselves, what they know about themselves. This is usually formed through experience and interaction with their environment and with other people. For example, young children may not know their family heritage. As they develop they will come to see themselves as belonging to certain social, cultural, religious, and political groups. The ideal self is how we think we should ideally be. Self-esteem is the value people put on their worth and this is usually based on comparing against the ideal self. Self-esteem tends to become more differentiated as children develop. An initial global evaluation in infancy gives way to more specific evaluations such as being good at sports or at mathematics or painting as the child develops.

High self-esteem gives rise to positive attitudes and makes children curious, willing to experiment, willing to take risks, accept challenges, and expect success – and nothing succeeds like it. Low self-esteem has a negative effect, making children incurious, defensive, expect failure, and avoid opportunities for change and learning. Self-esteem is said to influence how people behave, understand their world, attribute success and failure, and their attitudes to learning. Self-esteem depends on how a person is treated by others and how the person compares to others. It can change with new information and adjustment of ideals, and new comparison groups. How much of this is cause, how much effect and its real explanatory value have all been questioned. Some theorists (for example, Muijs and Reynolds 2001) argue that research has clearly established that good self-concepts and high self-esteem contribute to high achievement and that achievement in turn affects self-concept and self-esteem. Teachers are advised on the basis of this theory and evidence to have high expectations of pupils and build confidence by offering responsibilities, constructive, positive feedback and showing that pupils' contributions are valued. Above all they are encouraged to find ways of enabling all pupils to experience success.

Yet philosophers like Carr (2000) warn that such concepts remain educationally problematic and criticise official documents which suggest that the development of self-esteem should be an educational aim. Admittedly, some advocates of self-esteem do take great pains to reject the use of indiscriminate praise and to distinguish self-esteem from less desirable qualities like excessive pride, self-centredness or boastfulness. Critics also raise concerns about the focus on the individual and the little attention given to social relationships, pointing to research that does not give grounds for optimism that children with high self-esteem are necessarily more caring of others, for example.

Practical ideas for raising self-esteem abound and many suggestions need to be looked at critically, tending as they do towards a focus on the self and on indiscriminate praise. Other texts, however, do emphasise the importance of raising self-confidence as learners (Muijs and Reynolds 2001). Emotional literacy is a somewhat similar area. It has a high official priority and is given increasing attention in schools through circle time and other such activities. Again, however, philosophers have urged some caution. It is worth drawing attention in this context to the fact that psychologists have also investigated friendship patterns and age-related differences. There is much of interest for teachers here which can illuminate personal and social development in the primary classroom and the early years of secondary schooling (Fontana 1995).

CONSTRUCTIVISM

The idea of constructivist learning is a major aspect of both Piaget's and Vygotsky's thinking (see Slater and Bremner 2003). Piaget saw children as active, independent meaning makers who construct knowledge rather than just receive it, active agents in their own development through interaction with their environment (physical and social). They learn to adapt to their environment and become better able to understand and operate in their world. Piaget identified two main processes, assimilation (incorporating experiences into existing schemes of thinking) and accommodation (a process whereby a developing person changes thinking to handle new information). Piaget saw the learner as a young scientist actively constructing knowledge through experiment with the environment, instead of coming as a blank slate or empty vessel to the classroom, waiting to be filled with units of knowledge pre-packaged by the teacher. Understanding cannot be swallowed whole; ideas need to be digested to fit into or modify existing networks of concepts and learners need to be motivated to be active in this process.

This constructivist approach is a markedly different conception of teaching and learning from some traditional views, though we should also note that it does not necessarily preclude a significant role for the structured direct presentation of ideas. This is the mistake that the search for the one best way leads to. As Bruner (1996) put it, there are times when a computational or symbol processing view of the mind is appropriate even if the general framework is a constructivist one.

While Piaget emphasised the internal psychology of the individual mind, Vygotsky stressed the social context of learning. Learning, he argued is social in nature and children actively explore the social environment. In this theory, the link between thought and language is important since language is a social activity. From this perspective, (in contrast to that of Piaget) teaching can have a strong influence on development and so Vygotsky put much more emphasis on pedagogy – but not direct teaching so much as teaching in interaction with students' ideas in group-working contexts. Hence the importance Vygotskians place on pupil-pupil dialogue as well as pupil-teacher interaction.

A key term in Vygotsky's thought is the zone of proximal development – now commonly referred to as the zpd. This awkward term basically refers to the fact that there is generally a significant gap between what children can do on their own and what they can do with assistance. In learning or apprenticeship contexts with more experienced peers and adults, children gradually incorporate ideas into their developing schemas of thought and this enables them to do alone what before they could only do with assistance. If you have read Chapter 3 before tackling this one, you may already have realised that Vygotsky's theory suggests an important role for formative assessment in developing learning. Metacognition – awareness of your own thinking and strategies – is also important.

In marked contrast to Piaget's theory, for Vygotsky there was a very positive role for teaching in aiding development. Instead of waiting for signs of readiness teaching leads development by 'marching ahead of it through the zpd' (Moore 2000). Moore also suggests that Vygotsky's ideas imply that instead of working at a national curriculum level, pupils should be attempting, with the teacher's assistance, tasks beyond their current level of achievement. Piagetian influences have the danger of contributing to a self-fulfilling prophecy whereby pupils not yet seen to be ready confirm this by lack of achievement.

ADOLESCENCE

Both primary and secondary teachers can be expected to take a keen interest in theories of adolescent development. Striking facts are the big difference in the age of onset of puberty and the marked individual variations in developmental patterns and reactions. There is of course a danger of regarding adolescence as a time of problems for all that experiences it. Most in fact don't have significant problems.

In psychological terms, young people developing through adolescence can be considered to have a number of 'developmental tasks' to work through. Erikson for instance (see Fontana 1995) suggested adolescence was mainly concerned with identity versus role confusion – working out who they are, what they believe in, what they want to become. Modern texts emphasise cognition and social development as major areas along with issues of physical maturation, peer group membership, sexual relationships, autonomy from parents, identity (including sex roles), internalising moral values and orientation to career choices. Changes in body shape, size, hormones and complexion can affect body image and self-esteem sometimes causing embarrassment and confusion but often also pride and a sense of achievement.

These adolescent concerns partly define the pastoral issues teachers have to deal with and raise boundary issues for teachers between their role as teachers and more specialist ones in the area of advice and care. About 15 per cent of children reach the onset of puberty in primary school but there is a wide gap between those who mature early and those who reach puberty later. This can mean that, say, a drama or English class working on *Romeo and Juliet* can show a wide range of maturity in discussions about love and sex. For teachers and schools, clear boundaries can be important, as can effective administration, awareness of to whom pupils with particular concerns might be referred, and making sure to listen effectively to pupils. Schools serve many functions for pupils at the adolescent stage.

OTHER SCHOOLS OF PSYCHOLOGY

It would be wrong not to mention briefly in this chapter the potential insights of other schools of psychology, namely information-processing theory, social-learning theory and ecological models. These are discussed in good detail in most introductory psychology texts. Information-processing theory has had much to say about key school phenomena such as attention and memory (or the lack of these!); Bandura's social-learning theory has had an influence on ideas of teacher modelling; and Bronfenbrenner's ecological model can help teachers to put their observations of children and older pupils as developing persons into a wider social and environmental context (see for example, Slater and Bremner 2003).

Dominating much psychology in the past was research on intelligence, intelligence quotients (IQ) and the nature-nurture issue – the extent to which intelligence depends on heredity as opposed to environmental factors. These debates have resurfaced from time to time but the modern emphasis is on the notion of multiple intelligences, ways of acknowledging these and helping them flourish. Schooling is no longer dominated by IQ testing, although aptitude testing is flourishing in occupational selection and being discussed in relation to higher education. The main thrust in school, however, is on finding ways to develop not just identify talent, on the assumption that, whatever the role of nature as opposed to nurture, there remains enormous scope for improving learning in school and out. The longstanding influence of IQism in education, however, has meant that many school cultures are still tied to thinking in terms of general ability and ability grouping. But researchers like Donald McIntyre (see Dixon et al. 2004) argue strongly that the notion of general ability is not a fruitful one for the classroom and offer as an alternative the idea of 'transformational' learning without predetermined limits.

Teachers can gain confidence from knowing that their actions are in line with developmental theory and research on leaning. The fact of continuing controversy is part of the nature of the territory. Any useful theory will forbid some practices and commend others. All theory has implications for practice, however convoluted the reasoning chain. If every practice fits a theory, however, the theory becomes decorative only. The range of competing theories helps to develop deeper

5 SCHOOLS AND SOCIETY

Classroom teachers do not work in a social vacuum. The schools they teach in are organisations with particular characteristics which influence how teachers work. In turn, schools are part of local authority systems (or, for independent schools, private networks) and of wider national systems of education. National educational policies and what goes on in school are deeply affected by cultural, political, historical and other factors in the society at large. Furthermore, globalisation means that different national systems increasingly influence one another. Schools are expected to play an important role in society, contributing to the realisation of its aims, principles and values in connection with the economy, health, culture, social relations and other aspects. All this means that, to work effectively as professionals, teachers need a good understanding of how schools operate, of how wider social, economic and political issues influence national educational policies and what goes on in the classroom, and of what roles schools and teachers can play in response to them. The main aim of this chapter is to introduce you to the business of getting inside these questions and issues, and of working through their implications for your role and actions as a teacher.

To this end, three main topics of importance to practising teachers are explored. First, the question of equity and diversity is addressed. This includes attention to special educational needs as well as questions of race, class, gender and so on. This will provide some insight into how wider social issues and values affect educational thinking, policies and practice. Educational policies are not given or inevitable. They are the result of political and social movements and thinking, as well as thinking about the nature of education and its inherent values. Teachers have had, and continue to have, an important part to play in policy formation and in its practical working out in schools and classrooms.

Secondly, the sociology of classroom interaction is considered. Research from this perspective into working classrooms has provided a number of important insights for teachers about roles, relationships and management, the effects of assessment, and approaches to learning. Lastly, the process of transition between different stages of education – preschool to primary and primary to secondary – is considered. While in the UK there has tended to be a strong separation of the different stages of education, barriers are breaking down and there is much official concern and policy development, which is resulting in more teachers working across the transition points. An understanding of how the school system is structured and functions can illuminate these challenges teachers face and the impact of national policies on classroom practice.

These insights are important for understanding your role as a teacher. Of course, teachers alone cannot change educational systems or society. But to work well in them, and to contribute to their development, they need to understand how they operate; and teachers as a group can develop practices and a professional voice on these issues. This resonates with wider concerns relating to the idea of an activist teaching profession and touches on issues of major social importance. Such issues are of course open to different political views, values and solutions; and teachers will doubtless show as much diversity here as exists among the population in general.

EQUITY AND DIVERSITY

Special needs and inclusion

Many teacher training entrants (at least for primary teaching) come with a keen interest in, and not infrequently experience of, working with children with special needs, and some have a strong desire to specialise in this area after they have gained requisite experience in classroom teaching. It has a high national policy profile. Although many issues remain to be resolved, in recent years there have been major developments in policies and practice.

This is an area where accepted terminology frequently changes. Professional and pressure groups working in this field attach a great deal of importance to the terms used to describe various aspects and argue that the connotations and assumptions underlying particular terms have a significant effect on perceptions and attitudes. In the fight to overcome disadvantages new understandings emerge about obstacles to equity and sources of discrimination and the terms found acceptable by activists in the area change. Over the years this has happened frequently so that many terms used without demur not so long ago (and still found in older texts) are now frowned on as misguided, demeaning and likely to reinforce prejudice and continue unhelpful approaches. Teachers have to be sensitive to these issues and changes, though many will also point to the danger of excessive political correctness.

The category of special educational needs now refers to any identified needs for which special arrangements, resources or management are necessary above standard provision to ensure these needs are met. Examples of resource support might be the need for wheelchair access to a classroom or a laptop for someone with dyslexia. Different needs will also require particular forms of teaching support. It is considered important to include in the category of special needs both physically disabled learners and those with special intellectual, emotional and behavioural difficulties.

Learning difficulties are difficulties learners experience. It is important to realise that these may be temporary difficulties. Teachers should talk of pupils or children with special needs not special needs children or SEN pupils. The latter approach easily falls into the trap of labelling people and locating the problem in the individual, rather than directing attention to what society and schools can do and their responsibility to provide adequate support and to adapt the curriculum and teaching to the circumstances of the learner. This is what is known as the deficit model – assuming the problem, the deficiency, is in the individual not in the inadequate response of the school or society to the individual's circumstances. It is, unfortunately, very easy to fall into deficit model thinking and you should be critically alert to this possibility in your own essay and exam writing and reflections in your placement teaching file. Children whose first language is not English should not be regarded as having a learning difficulty, however, although they will have particular support needs.

Another important point is to see the range of needs and difficulties in learning as a continuum with a necessity for professional judgement as to when separate provision is required. It is not a matter of hard boundaries between groups of learners. There are moderate and severe difficulties, temporary and more permanent conditions. There is a general need in education to rethink unhelpful traditional assumptions, arrangements and practices. The aim should be to enable not disable, and to adopt a social model not just a medical or deficit model. In the social model of disability, society is seen as disabling the person through its provision and organisation. This social model is linked to human rights thinking, policy development and legislation.

Inclusion policies involve the presumption of mainstream education for all children. It is part of the commitment to higher standards for all learners. Schools are expected to develop their cultures, policies and practices to include pupils. While the policy assumes that nearly all children with special needs can be successfully included in mainstream education, each child's interests must be safeguarded and mainstream education will not always be right for every child. But because it is not considered appropriate at one stage this does not mean it may not be considered appropriate later. All children require access to the national curriculum and arrangements need to be made to provide this somehow, at an appropriate level. Debate among committed professionals and others continues about how far this is possible and desirable. However, inclusion is now a firmly accepted principle of governmental social and educational policy and the emphasis is shifting towards a closer analysis of how this principle can be realised in actual schools and classrooms.

Behaviour modification techniques which were prominent some years ago are tending to give way to interactive, person-to-person approaches to teaching. Individual learning plans (IEPS) are seen by many as an important development though they do need time for monitoring and supporting them properly. It is important that pupils with English as an additional language are not just given simple tasks.

Mainstream schools now have significant responsibilities and it is considered the earlier special needs are recognised the better and that overcoming difficulties in language and mathematics is crucial for further educational progress. But this does not mean only teaching through formal mathematics and language. Teaching needs to be across the curriculum.

Racism

The issue of racism is discussed below as another extended example of the issues teachers face in realising principles of inclusion and equity in professional action. While many of the points made here about racism, and earlier about disability, apply also to other forms of discrimination, each aspect also has its unique problems. Areas of discrimination need to be considered both separately and together.

Teacher training entrants usually express strong commitment to being fair, treating pupils equally and not discriminating on grounds of class, race, gender, sexuality or ethnicity. Discrimination in various forms persists, however, in schools and society. Hence playing an effective role here requires some hard thinking by teachers – a close examination of ideas and facts, recent history and of professional action open to teachers.

Racism is an ideology or belief about the superiority of one race over another and racist actions are those which discriminate on grounds of race. In tackling the issue of racism and education, it is helpful to bear in mind the three kinds of racism that have been distinguished (see for example, Thompson 1998). Personal racism refers to antagonistic or negative outlooks or behaviour towards persons of a different ethnic group. It contributes to inequalities and injustice, particularly if individuals acting in a racist way are in positions of some power. Cultural racism is when a particular culture perceives itself as superior to others. A dominant culture can impose its patterns, assumptions and values on others, often unconsciously, and these are assumed to be the natural ways of everyday living. This too can lead to inequalities among diverse groups in a plural society. Institutional racism refers to the collective failure of an organisation such as a school, university, or police force to provide an equitable service to people because of their colour, culture, or ethnicity. It can be detected in procedures, attitudes and behaviour which result in discrimination through unwitting prejudice, ignorance, thoughtlessness and stereotyping. Institutional racism persists when organisations fail to recognise that it exists and to change policies and procedures to eliminate it. Leadership can be a crucial factor here.

The QTS standards in England (and equivalents elsewhere) require teachers to set high expectations for all pupils, providing equal opportunities for all. This includes pupils with special needs, disabilities, from all social and cultural backgrounds, different ethnic and linguistic groups, including travellers, refugees and asylum seekers. They should ensure they do not unintentionally discriminate. There are now firm legal regulations concerning racial discrimination. Legislation in 1976 made it illegal to discriminate on grounds of race, colour, nationality or ethnic origin in the UK. Furthermore, the Race Relations (Amendment) Act 2000 laid down that local authorities and teachers had a positive and legal duty not only to eliminate unlawful racial discrimination but also to promote equal opportunities and good relationships between people from different racial groups. Taking these principles and legal requirements seriously implies being committed to understanding why discrimination continues to exist and what steps can be taken to help counter it, and becoming aware of the details of good classroom and school practice in this area.

As you begin to explore this area in your training you should have a chance to examine the assumptions that have underpinned various responses to black immigration in the last half century. There have been three main phases – assimilation, multiculturalism and anti-racism – and anti-racism has now been linked with policies in other areas of discrimination under the general umbrella of equity and inclusion. Initial policies and attitudes assuming assimilation into British society gradually gave way to multiculturalism. This was a first step in recognising the plural society Britain always has been and now most obviously is. But the multicultural phase was unsatisfactory in that significant racist behaviour continued within schools and society and multiculturalism too often became a tokenistic celebration of diversity without addressing the key issues of discrimination, inequality and violence against black people. Anti-racist education polices were fought for and eventually officially recognised. Many issues remain to be resolved, however.

Implementation of equity policies remains piecemeal and liable to neglect as other priorities emerge. Often the main focus is on recording racist incidents and supporting pupils with English as an additional language but goes little further. Overt discrimination has been reduced but subtle racism persists. Action often appears to stop short when real equality measures are suggested which threaten privileged positions. Some schools are reluctant to discuss the benefits of race equality for ethnic minority pupils and the positive effects on the majority population. Complacency about racism was shaken by the Macpherson Report (1999; Stephen Lawrence Inquiry). Legislation followed and schools are now expected to put race equality into practice in a pro-active as well as responsive way and to embed race equality in teaching, learning and curriculum and the wider aspects of schooling. Where discrimination is found they are required to take steps to remove it.

Recent studies have demonstrated that hitherto teachers in training have been ill prepared with respect to core principles and examples of good practice. They remain unsure about whether to highlight issues of racism in school contexts or to discuss them with pupils, are not confident about terms (preferring to use softer words like ethnic and inclusion instead of racism or anti-racism) and often retain misguided assumptions about the values of minorities. Likewise some pupils feel inhibited, although where well-organised opportunities exist and they have some assurance that they will not be singled out, they talk confidently about such issues. Research studies have also highlighted the effects of racism on reducing self-confidence and the negative effects it has on school climate, pupil behaviour and learning performance, school community relationships, participation and educational outcomes.

Anti-racist education is a necessary component in all schools, even those with hardly any ethnic minority pupils. Minority ethnic pupils can have worse experiences of racism in mainly white schools, the value of cultural and ethnic diversity is often underplayed and minority pupils are discouraged from expressing important aspects of their identity and cultural heritage, for example language or religion. In such schools there is sometimes little awareness of the extent of racist discrimination and harassment in the local communities and beyond.

Some schools have worked hard over recent years to create an ethos which welcomes all and confronts racism. They ensure good communication with parents who do not speak/read English and recognise the range of community languages. They use positive minority ethnic images and role models. They have firm and consistent measures to address racism in the school and playground, and involve all staff, governors and parents in supporting the anti-racist approaches taken in the school. Citizenship now receives a high profile in British schools. It has an important part to play in developing attitudes to equality in a plural society. There are now many useful curriculum materials on citizenship, inclusion and equity to aid teachers and examples of effective policies and community projects on which schools and teachers can build (see further, **www.education.ac.uk/ceres**).

Other aspects of equity and diversity

Any detailed consideration of issues of gender and sexual discrimination would show that these areas have several features
in common with the case of racism but also issues that are
specific to each. In relation to gender schools' attitudes and
practices concerning curriculum choices and educational
attainment remain important and problematic; and in relation to sexuality questions of school and class ethos, bullying
and so on need to be addressed. There is a great deal of useful
reading now available on these issues, including practical
advice for classroom teachers in their day-to-day roles (see for
example, Cole 2000; Browne and Haylock 2004).

Although we have already considered two extended examples in the area of equity and diversity, it is important to say
something briefly about other aspects of discrimination.
Inequalities in educational attainment matter for teachers
because they affect the individual life chances of pupils.
Education systems tend to develop in a way that reflects the
inequalities present in the society in general. Discrimination
and disadvantage lead to inequalities of access to education
and thus further disadvantage and injustice, preventing the
realisation of societal aims such as equality of opportunity. At
the same time, education is often seen as a means of reducing
inequalities and as having great potential for enhancing living
standards and social development.

Social class
Despite policies aimed to reduce them, social class differences
in opportunities and outcomes have tended to persist. Across
the UK, for example, there are still big differences between the
top and bottom socio-economic groups (managers and professionals as opposed to manual workers) in the number of
qualifications gained at age sixteen. Research generally continues to demonstrate that, while attainments in school
leaving examinations have increased overall, the relative gaps
in performance between social groups have barely altered
over recent decades. There are, however, some interesting

exceptions (see Tinklin and Raffe 1999) which point the way to possible policy developments to reduce class inequalities.

Poverty remains a major source of underachievement. Teachers can inform their teaching in addressing these issues by developing a good understanding of how inequalities work. This is not, however, a matter of learning some fashionable slogans and policy rhetoric. Rather it requires deeper, critical study of the facts of disadvantage, of how various factors prevent high achievement, and a sensitivity to the way in which the hidden curriculum can help reproduce inequities in achievement and in society generally.

It is also important to develop a good understanding of the insights that research is beginning to bring into the kinds of teaching approaches, local strategies and large-scale programmes that are proving successful in reducing inequalities. Historical studies of schooling (for example, Paterson 2003) can shed light on issues such as how a system can reconcile aims for promoting democratic educational and social principles with the need for occupational and cultural selection. Paterson argues that in Scotland a commitment to common educational institutions has gone along with a rather traditionally academic conception of schooling and the question is how far this is the best approach for the twenty-first century.

At a broader level, the study of the sociology of education can make a significant contribution to raising awareness of the ways in which the problems of inequality in a given society interact with and reflect international issues of economic development, globalisation, human rights and environmental concerns.

THE SOCIOLOGY OF THE CLASSROOM

In addition to the issue of equity already discussed, sociology is able to offer teachers a wealth of insights into teaching and education which can illuminate the teacher's role and stimulate further professional development. Only a flavour of what is available can be provided here but this may serve to stimulate further investigation in relevant texts such as Meighan and Siraj-Blatchford (1997). One main focus of research in the sociology of education has been classroom interaction. There have been studies of power relations between teachers and pupils and of the effect of teacher expectations on pupil performance (the danger of negative expectations becoming self-fulfilling prophecies). Sociologists have also explored the unconscious, subtle socialisation into conformity with particular norms and values (which critics claim are often linked to class and economic ideologies) through curriculum and teaching methods from nursery schooling upwards. Other studies have investigated the ways in which learning tasks are interpreted and negotiated by pupils (a certain ambiguity enabling pupils to have more control of work rates) together with analyses of the various roles teachers and pupils can take on in the theatre of the classroom ('lion tamers', 'sherpas', 'class clowns' and so on). Mention should also be made of the general insights into the social realities of classroom life illustrated so well in Philip Jackson's classic *Life in Classrooms* (1968). In relation to assessment, there are broad analyses of its role in society and its effects on curriculum and teaching (Broadfoot 1999) and of how pupils experience it in classrooms (Filer and Pollard 2000).

There are also more fundamental critiques of the roles of schools in society, of patterns of schooling and of government polices on performance management, curriculum control and so on. Another rich sociological seam has been the study of 'critical pedagogy' from writers like Friere (see Friere and Macedo 1998) who has influenced wider thinking and educational action, and contributed important insights relevant for day-to-day classroom teaching in connection with dialogue between teacher and pupil and the role of teacher as facilitator. A sustained critique of the ideologies and class biases underlying typical curriculum content and policies has been produced by Apple (2004).

It can thus be seen that educational sociology has enormous scope and potential for illuminating the teacher's role and issues facing schools and society today. You should certainly take what opportunities arise on your course to explore areas of interest and to develop your understanding of this important dimension. Different teacher education courses are likely to put differing emphases on particular aspects, relating in part to staff expertise and specialisms. No initial training course is going to be able to provide a comprehensive study of the sociology of education. Sociology of education has of late been more neglected in teacher training than its potential relevance and insights warrant, although it is now reappearing through Education Studies modules.

Needless to say, one fact of life here is the range of sociological schools or perspectives. These offer contrasting accounts of how education systems work, their problems and solutions. At first, it can be off-putting to encounter lists of different sociological perspectives, usually with jargonised labels; but society is complex, as is its relationship to education, and many introductory sociological texts (Giddens 2001, is an excellent example) explain key ideas in a lucid and stimulating way. Giddens in fact argues that the diversity of perspectives is a sign of the vitality of the discipline. Sociology offers challenging perspectives, explanations and understanding of events and behaviour in classrooms and schools. It identifies factors which need to be taken into account if educational aims and wider goals for education and social transformation are to be realised.

THE PROCESS OF TRANSITION

It is important for teachers to appreciate the nature of the transition process at key stages in the education system. This is because pupils voice concerns, because transfer can create a hiatus in learning, and because studies have shown the positive role teachers can play to reduce the problems pupils experience. The national curriculum in England, Wales and Northern Ireland and the 5–14 programme in Scotland were designed in part to ensure clear progression, but present arrangements have not proved a full answer. Recent national curriculum documents strongly emphasise the need to think of the school curriculum as a whole, as a coherent system from three to eighteen (for example, Scottish Executive 2004). Study of this issue also provides insights into how school systems work and the impact of structural features on teaching and learning.

Boys appear to be the most vulnerable group and they voice concerns about bullying, exams, and relations with teachers. Girls' concerns are more often about lunches, missing the bus, detention. They tend to have more close friends. About 40 per cent of pupils fail to make expected progress in the first year of transition to secondary school, while for nearly 7 per cent there is a serious hiatus. Most, however, soon settle into the transition. Individuals show varied reactions to change. Some embrace it while others shy away. Transition obviously is a process which involves breaking away form one context and integrating into another and a number of arrangements and activities can help pupils make such transitions. Among them are buddy systems, effective transfer information and bridging projects.

In Britain we tend to assume there is a natural difference between primary and secondary education. Many other areas (like Scandinavia and Eastern Europe), however, now have longstanding traditions of a basic school from about six to fifteen and then a clear break as pupils move to upper secondary education. This makes for a smoother transition between ten and fourteen years of age into specialist subject teaching and from having a single class teacher to having a range of subject teachers. Also, in some countries, pre-school starts at six or seven, not five. Viewed in historical and comparative perspective, abrupt transfer to secondary at eleven is no law of nature, and in retrospect looks something of an evolutionary mistake in the development of the UK educational systems.

The fresh-start issue

Secondary teachers tend to underestimate pupil attainments at transition, while primary teachers tend to overestimate.

Secondary teachers are often very cautious about primary assessment information and often have a strong belief in a fresh start and in judging from close inspection of pupils, once they see them at work in class. They often imply that basic skills are more important than subject content for primary school. Secondary teachers, however, have the challenge of getting to know several classes of pupils and to plan individually for them. Primary attainment data are potentially very valuable for secondary teachers at the transition.

The way forward

The problems of transitions have proved much more difficult to resolve than was assumed at the advent of national curricula. Good liaison arrangements can ease transitions and the quality of transfer data can be improved. The idea of a fresh start is not wholly misguided, but it needs to be an informed fresh start. Policy and practice across transitions will clearly need to continue to develop to meet new research evidence, to compensate for structural problems in the system and to respond to the diversity of learners, their development patterns and reactions to transition.

Learning to handle change should not be seen as a problem, a distraction from the core business of the school in making progress in literacy, numeracy and academic knowledge. It is itself at the centre of personal and social development, a context for some very valuable learning. Fresh starts are part of growing up and progress in learning is often far from linear.

Liaison by itself, however, is unlikely to prove sufficient. A deeper dialogue is required recognising the deep-seated differences in the culture of thinking about curriculum, pedagogy and assessment between the two sectors, despite the fact that there is no real justification for such a gulf. Some mutual reconceptualisation of the transition in terms of curriculum structure, pedagogy and assessment seems required. A balanced approach to reconciling the differences across the transition both from primary to secondary could itself enhance the quality and outcomes of education in both sectors. Much the same applies to the nursery-primary transition, though here the sustained research and development work covering early education as a whole has led to much less of a gulf.

PART II
Professional Practice

6   LEARNING FROM PLACEMENT

In undergraduate teacher training, placement in school takes up from a quarter to a third of the total time. In PGCE courses it is at least half the time, and in some school-based programmes over three quarters. Teaching students naturally see placement as the heart of any teacher education programme, where they put into practice theory and methods of teaching learned at university. It is the area where they judge they most need to succeed and the place where all other professional learning comes to fruition. Succeeding here certainly is vital, and to do so you need to involve yourself fully in what is undoubtedly the central task – learning to plan, conduct and evaluate teaching in the class or classes to which you are assigned. But to get the most out of placement you need to approach it from a broad perspective, taking into account your training course as a whole.

Placement is not just a matter of practising classroom teaching. It aims to be a much richer and deeper professional learning experience. On placement you are also learning to become an active member of a school staff, and gaining experience of a teacher's wider professional roles and responsibilities. This includes communicating with parents, taking part in staff development and school development planning, contributing to extra-curricular activities and collaborating with specialist teachers to support learning. Much more is involved than just subject or classroom teaching. Moreover, placement is not just about practice: it is a very good context for deepening your understanding of theory and gathering data for professional assignments which you write up for university. You need to appreciate these wider aims and take full advantage of opportunities that arise for broad professional learning and observing exemplification in a school setting of all the professional standards.

There are several possible placement patterns. Placements can be short or long, stage-related or across a school, singly with a class teacher or as a group placement involving several students working with a number of classes. In England and Wales you will commonly have a designated mentor (an experienced member of staff, possibly a class teacher) who has been nominated to support and guide your learning in the school setting. In Scotland, you will be supervised by the class teacher (primary) or several teachers (secondary), but there will also be someone senior in the school formally responsible for managing student teachers. The ways in which students are allocated to school placements and the partnerships between training providers and school authorities vary considerably. In recent years, partnership arrangements have been developing rapidly. You should find clear agreements about allocation procedures, quality assurance, support and the roles of the various actors in the situation – the university or course provider, the educational authority, the particular school, and the student teacher.

Schools vary a great deal in size and you need to get to know how they operate as institutions and as communities. The majority of secondary schools are large and can appear bureaucratic in operation. Some primary schools are very small communities, though increasingly with good links into wider local and national policy developments and support systems. Don't assume that schools will operate like offices, the civil service, universities, or whatever institutions you are familiar with. Don't look askance for example, if you find teachers do not spend their breaks in the staff room discussing educational ideas and policies, or if they seem unfamiliar with some ideas you have encountered in university. At break time the staff will be doing just that – having a well-deserved break from teaching and its concerns; and perhaps letting off steam about pupils, policies and life outside school. You have not wandered into an educational seminar. Staff development sessions are where teachers discuss educational ideas and practices. In short, learn to understand how schools work, their formal and informal networks, and schools' characteristics as communities.

In approaching a placement there is one crucial fact to bear in mind. While the class teacher will play an important role in helping you to succeed, his or her main concern and responsibility will rightly be with the education of the pupils. You at first, equally naturally, will be tempted to focus on your own performance and professional learning as you try to find your feet. An important goal, however, is to also learn to focus on the educational needs of the pupils, and thus begin to develop the perspective of a practising teacher. The pupils are not guinea pigs; they are there to learn, and their parents will want to be sure they are doing so. You need to see yourself as having responsibility for this during your placement, under the teacher's direction.

Once you establish a good relationship, by showing a positive attitude and willingness to work hard, most teachers will prove very supportive and go the extra mile to help you do well. But don't assume that you are the main focus in their day-to-day work, even for the duration of your placement. Apart from their own teaching, they may have other commitments and responsibilities in school, for example in relation to curriculum development. You will be an extra responsibility, which they will take seriously. Aim to prove an asset, not a burden, while also learning with your teacher's guidance and support.

There may well be occasions when you will find things are not quite as expected. Your best response to whatever faces you on placement is to say to yourself: 'Here is the context. What can I best learn in this situation?' It may not be quite what you hoped. It may be that what you learn is to work effectively with an awkward colleague or with scarce resources, or with greater independence than envisaged in the placement guidelines because your teacher is ill and there is only a supply teacher for the class. If any of this happens, resolve to be positive, take advice from senior staff and use it as a professional learning experience. It could turn out to be a more valuable experience than if things had gone according to plan. You will need to cope with similar situations sometime in your career.

ASPECTS TO CONSIDER

School staff you come into contact with during placement will inevitably size you up as a potential member of the profession, a possible colleague, while also expecting you to act like a (good) student teacher. The main principle is to strike a balance between being over confident and too timid. Try to understand the culture of the school and how working professionals cope and get support from the context and its activities.

On your introductory visit, make sure you are well organised, well informed and open to ideas – ready to run with them but not naively over the top in enthusiasm. Be positive but not pushy. On your first meeting don't focus on your entitlements, such as time to plan or to go back to the university. Remember how important first impressions and a good start can be and ask about what is expected and how you can contribute. Don't assume the teachers can answer your hundred questions immediately. They will not necessarily be up to date with all you have learned in the university. Think what you can expect to learn from busy teachers and judge when and how much to ask.

Every placement context is different. Don't make assumptions or criticisms based on your last placement. Find out how your new placement school works. Think about dress codes; take advice and on your first day dress slightly formally, and then observe the range and norms of your placement school. Play an appropriate role in the staff room. You are there as a guest and trying to operate as a temporary, junior member of staff. Don't hide away in your class, but be one of the first to move there when the bell goes. Don't dominate the conversation but join in naturally.

In some contexts you will be expected to attend staff meetings, in others, not. You will find that many staff development sessions are excellent learning experiences. Schools occasionally need to have internal discussion about issues without outsiders present. Perhaps they don't consider a particular issue relevant to you. Go with the flow here. If the school does not think it appropriate for you to attend a given session, find something useful to do, for example resource preparation or mounting a wall display.

Concern for health and safety is absolutely fundamental, even as a student teacher. Never be careless about this. You will not be unsupervised but do be pro-active in finding out about fire drills and other health and safety policies and procedures. On a placement you also need to pay attention to your own health. At first it can prove tiring as you prepare for the next day and write up your teaching file each evening. You may find, until you become acclimatised, that you quickly pick up all the coughs, colds and whatever is circulating among the pupils. The best solution is to build up your immunity by a healthy diet and exercise and by managing your time effectively.

Placement, like everyday teaching, is typically a matter of ups and downs with perhaps a plateau in between, rather than a steady progression in competence. One day things go well, the next day the reverse. A secondary subject lesson that works brilliantly with one class can fall flat when repeated to another at the same stage. Everyone experiences days in teaching when nothing seems to go as they hoped. All this is natural in highly interactive professions like teaching and teachers learn to take the rough with the smooth.

Put effort into building a good relationship with the teachers you work with. Aim for clear communication from the start. If something isn't clear, ask politely. If things start going wrong try to sort it out sooner rather than later. Ask advice from your university tutor if unsure and try to see the teacher's perspective. Collaborating with a teacher is very much a matter of give and take. Feedback on teaching from the teacher may only be in his or her spare time. You can't always expect the teacher to look at your lesson plans in the way that your tutor might. He or she can, however, offer advice as an experienced practitioner in that context – about how the pupils might respond, how long they will take to get through it, how effective the resources will prove and so on. Your university tutor is likely to focus on other aspects as well, such as clarity of learning outcomes, assessment criteria and links to teaching ideas and wider theory.

There is a dilemma in training that all student teachers have to come to terms with. On the one hand, you are expected to be a fully reflective practitioner and in the university you will be encouraged to look critically at ideas, research and practice. On placement, however, you must always remember you are a visitor in school and a novice (but doubtless very promising) teacher. It is fatal to make overt criticisms of the school, its policies or teaching. It is easy to criticise teaching but it is difficult to accomplish teaching effectively day by day. Learn to be generous in observing others' teaching. You won't know fully the background, underlying issues, pressures and tensions. Focus your public criticisms on your own teaching until you are qualified.

You will have to consider your own developing teaching style in relation to that of the teacher of your class. You cannot act like a clone. You need to use a style that suits your individuality, while adapting sufficiently to your teacher's approach to the class.

A number of balances need to be struck by students undertaking school placements (Hayes 2004) and indeed most aspects of your work on placement can be so viewed. You need to become alert to the difference between being confident and calmly assertive and insistently demanding; showing initiative and being pushy; failing to exploit a school's resources and thoughtlessly squandering what the teacher has carefully gathered for a forthcoming project; coming well-prepared but flexible and always having a last minute rush to prepare; being mature and realistic and being worldly wise and cynical; being a help and being interfering; being chatty and interested and being verbose and intrusive.

TUTOR VISITS AND ASSESSMENTS

Details vary across courses within the UK, although there is an underlying similarity of basic principles and features. Find out the particular arrangement pertaining to your course – how many tutor visits, how many formal observations and assessments by the school and what you need to do to meet the standards.

A visiting tutor will normally have to do several things: talk with your teacher(s) and some senior member of staff; examine your teaching file; watch you teach; discuss with you and offer feedback; write up an assessment form (this may be completed later); consult briefly again with your teacher and possibly other staff before leaving. This means that in a two-hour visit your tutor may only see you teach for 30–40 minutes. In a half-day visit you will probably be observed for longer. Research evidence suggests that a tutor can get a good view of your teaching in about twenty minutes. It may be more productive to watch sections of different lessons, instead of a single, full one. You will naturally want to do your best for your tutor. But aim to provide a regular lesson, well prepared and resourced, not a special show piece. Students are sometimes tempted to resource these lessons extravagantly. Your tutor and the school will be more impressed if your lesson imaginatively uses regular resourcing, is well thought out and taught, and is something you could deliver day in, day out.

THEORY AND PRACTICE

Practice alone is not usually the best way to learn. It may be one good way to start, but being thrown in at the deep end and left to sink or swim is no help to most learners; besides, some may drown. The time when students were expected to learn all the theory in college and then put it into practice in school with the emphasis on classroom teaching skills has long gone. A good deal of current practice in school stems from staff development initiatives led by consultants and others who have taken research studies and ideas and produced practical guidance based on them. Your university studies are the equivalent of this in initial training. In both cases there is a link between theory and practice. Schools are sites for research and development, not just for implementing ideas developed in universities and policy centres, very important though that is.

Teacher education institutions aim to provide the most up-to-date training on a range of aspects, including curriculum, teaching, ICT and other resources. Inevitably, in some schools, resources and current practice will not make it possible to implement all the ideas learned in the university. Besides, schools will have valuable ideas of their own from which you can learn much. For these reasons there will be some unavoidable differences between your university teaching and the practical context of a particular school. Universities also have a duty to contribute to educational development through research, independent thinking and critique of government policy and to introduce you to these perspectives on education in schools.

Tutors and schools will provide formative feedback to help you learn. Effective advice is prompt, focused and constructive and will encourage you to take responsibility, with support, for your continuing development. Where placement performance is no longer graded A to E but just Pass/Fail (an increasing trend), you will find a more open professional learning atmosphere, while still having to meet fully the standards of the placement.

Professional roles and responsibilities have widened following a range of policy developments and entitlements, and teamwork is an ever more important aspect of work in schools and classrooms. In a primary classroom there may well be several adults alongside the teacher – such as parent helpers, classroom assistants, special needs auxiliaries, nursery nurses. Secondary teachers need to liaise with other colleagues and support staff. Placement provides opportunities to engage in such team-working situations.

PLANNING YOUR TEACHING

Good planning provides confidence as a professional, is highly valued by teachers and schools and you'll notice the difference in the response to your teaching by pupils and staff when your planning is really first-rate. The standards put a major emphasis on planning effectively and your ability here will be judged by your written plans as well as actual teaching.

To get off to a good start, you need to know why planning is important, understand its principles and methods, learn how to link your individual lesson plans to your teachers' medium- and longer-term plans, and learn to plan for the medium-term yourself. Students usually begin by learning to plan single lessons, often part of a teacher's wider planning, then learn to develop longer sequences of progressive learning. National curriculum guidelines and exemplification, central planning and resourcing by schools, and websites from which you can download ready-made plans have dramatically changed the planning scene. In addition to curriculum centralisation, this reflects efforts to cut down teachers' planning workloads so that they can concentrate on teaching itself.

As a trainee, you will still have limited teaching experience and a full lesson plan is partly a substitute for experience. As experience grows you'll be able to reduce the extent of written planning. It is important to set yourself a target of becoming less dependent on written plans over your course for as a qualified teacher you will not have time to write full plans for all lessons. Make sure to develop a sound foundation by thorough written planning first, however, or things may rapidly fall apart.

Lesson planning should be seen as a discipline which gives direction and motivation to teaching. In preparing your first lessons you will need an outline script to support you – notes to guide the introduction, development and conclusion of the lesson, together with any key questions or information you intending to convey, and notes on resources. You also need to write down what you expect pupils to learn (the learning outcomes), important aspects of teaching and learning and how you will assess their understanding. Some of these lesson planning aspects can at first prove quite difficult to grasp. The following explanation should help you to quickly master the essential points. There is no set order of planning and most teachers use an interactive approach to the various elements described in a linear fashion below.

Learning activity

A useful first stage is to clarify the learning activity the children will be undertaking. This could be writing a story, conducting a science experiment, appraising historical documents and so on. A concise description of the activity will help you focus on other planning decisions. Students were once expected to show that they could create their own resources. The emphasis now, however, is on accessing and adapting published resources and deploying them intelligently for a particular class. Your teaching plans also need to be informed by school curriculum policies.

Outcomes

Next, you need to specify learning outcomes for the activity. It is vital to distinguish what you want pupils to learn from what you want them to do. Learning outcomes are clear statements about what you hope they will learn from the activity. Don't merely write down what pupils will do (like 'write a summary' or 'solve five problems'); pinpoint what they will learn, for example how to describe accurately or how to apply a certain problem-solving strategy. Work at this distinction and it will pay off well. Modern teachers need to think out clear learning outcomes, not just think in terms of activities.

Planning assessment

You will now be able to plan assessment. Consider what evidence will convince you they have learnt what you intended and devise some way of obtaining this evidence. Will it be by what pupils say, write or do? Will it be by observing the activity, examining the end products or application exercises? Don't become bogged down in rituals (like routine worksheets or tests) but think out for yourself the best way to assess the intended learning.

Teaching and learning

Along with a clear activity, expected outcomes and assessment you need to consider teaching and learning. Don't unthinkingly adopt some routine strategy but work out the best way to help your pupils learn. In some contexts, national guidance specifies teaching approaches and lesson structures but you need to use such prescriptions critically and imaginatively. Good teaching depends on judgement and expertise, not mechanical compliance to official prescription.

There is a range of possible lesson planning structures with different mixes of plenary sessions, group and individual work (see Hayes 2003) which you can expect to be advised about in relation to your particular subject or stage of schooling. Advice will doubtless also be forthcoming, with examples, on approaches to differentiating work as appropriate to meet the range of needs and attainments in your class. This is usually based on five possible approaches: by task, outcome, support, resources and time.

Pupil perspective

Now think the lesson through from the viewpoint of a pupil, envisioning its expected flow, the time it will require, the organization, distribution, management and collection of resources, and safety issues. With experience you will judge better how long it will take the pupils, what questions they will ask, difficulties they might encounter. But in your first placement check with the teacher if what you have planned is sensible.

Modern thinking urges teachers to provide work that is challenging but attainable, to share the learning outcomes and the big picture with the pupils, instead of keeping them in the dark, and to cater for visual, auditory and kinaesthetic learners by a range of examples and presentation approaches. Aim to devise learning experiences that sustain attention and motivate. Break the material down to make it meaningful to the learners. There's a wealth of ideas on the web (for example **www.emaths.co.uk** and **www.hamilton-trust.org.uk**) and in teachers' magazines to tap into (taking care to adapt for your context) and so quickly get some good lessons under your belt.

Into action

To implement your plan, ensure the class is settled, briefly remind them what they had learned in the previous lesson in the sequence, then put your plan into action flexibly. Keep an eye on the progress of the lesson and conditions of working. Find ways of involving pupils and giving them responsibilities. Make sure to bring the lesson to a proper close. Medium-term planning involves developing coherent and progressive teaching sequences. These are important curriculum principles. You may find it best to begin with an overall shape or aim for a unit of work and then to plan individual lessons. Alternatively, start from an individual lesson and build up a sequence from there.

Trainee teachers often cover too much in a single lesson. Experience usually teaches you to do less in more depth, ensuring stronger learning and better overall progress. However, there are also pressures for coverage and you need to learn to balance all this as you develop experience in medium- and longer-term planning. Above all, make sure you plan to engage pupils in worthwhile learning activities.

Your Teaching File is a crucial placement document. It serves three functions. It is a working file for your own planning, evaluation and professional learning; it is a tool for communicating with the school, teachers and tutors; and it is a way of accounting for teaching you have undertaken. This means it needs to be clear, well organised, flexible, kept up to date and manageable. Mentors, tutors and others will examine your file as evidence of progress in meeting the standards. They will be impressed not by bulk but by the quality and organisation of its content.

CLASS MANAGEMENT

Class management is always of prime concern for trainee teachers. Everyone is concerned about it: parents, the public, inspectors, placement tutors, even pupils. Fortunately, there have been significant policy and training developments in recent years designed to help new teachers meet the challenges they can undoubtedly face in this area. Most schools are now expected to have clear behaviour management policies so that the teacher has a firm system of support and pupils know what the rules are, what behaviour is acceptable and what sanctions will be operated if they misbehave. Moreover, there is now a wide range of practical texts and video/DVD/CD-ROM on class discipline which can enable student teachers to develop a strong foundation of practical management techniques.

However, unless alongside all this you have thought through certain attitudes and values relating to your role as a teacher, you will struggle with discipline. The foundation of good class management is to have a clear conception of your responsibility as a teacher to help pupils learn. You are not in class just to be the pupils' friend and certainly not their pal (they have their own already). Effective explaining and questioning will count for naught unless it is complemented by equally skilled class management. Without good control your pupils will not be able to learn. Yet you need to exercise control in a way that maintains and develops good relationships with the class and is informed by sound educational values. Unfortunately, this is where some new teachers do get stuck, giving priority to friendly relations over learning and control. All three go together, however. As a teacher you need to see yourself not only as an expert on the curriculum, teaching and learning but also on ensuring the safe and orderly conduct of teaching and learning and as committed to good relationships with learners.

You need to realise that children will inevitably test you out. This does not mean they are badly brought up; they are just human and not in school of their own free will. Besides, not all learning activities are exciting. The sociology of classroom life leads them to test you. It is how they find out exactly what the rules and boundaries are. You can't just announce a set of rules and expect obedience. Children need to interpret them in concrete terms by seeing what level of noise counts as 'working reasonably quietly' and so on. If you are a soft touch they will soon run over you. If you become authoritarian, relationships and the class ethos will quickly deteriorate. You need to be calm, confident, vigilant, firm, consistent and determined to follow through. Try to view class management from the perspective of pupils' personal and social development and ensure you have a clear, well-prepared teaching plan matched to the needs of the class and differentiated as appropriate.

The important thing is not to let discipline get off to a bad start. It is very difficult to recover control once lost. The problem is that some student teachers think that during the first week or so they can just be friendly, until they are in charge on their own. But in school you are always in a management context, and pupils will be checking you out from the start. When you are in charge of the class or a group, you need to show initiative in management, even if the teacher is in the background; but of course don't overreach by correcting a child when the teacher is there and clearly supervising that child. Don't think that it will be easier when you have the class entirely to yourself as a qualified teacher. It is likely to be more difficult. Admittedly, as a student, you need to manage the class in the context of the teacher's overall approach, which can be a challenge but usually is a help to you. You need to exert your own discipline and can't assume they will obey you as they do the teacher. You don't see the careful groundwork the teacher put in the weeks or months before you arrived. Be assured there was a great deal.

Try to develop a clear view about what pupils like in teachers. Research evidence suggests they prefer teachers who are slightly strict because their experience shows that they learn and enjoy school best under such regimes. Humour can also be important, along with skill in explaining and provision of interesting lessons. Learn about how to develop a good class ethos by discussing rules and celebrating pupils' success.

Merrett and Wheldall (1990) have shown that by far the main problems of discipline in schools are persistent but minor ones like talking out of turn, hindering other children and out-of-seat behaviour, rather than outright disobedience or physical violence. Yet these minor problems are very common and they can wear teachers down. The researchers argue, however, that these discipline problems are readily amenable to positive behaviour management techniques based on the psychology of B. F. Skinner (see Chapter 4). The strong national commitment to implementation of inclusion policies makes it important to learn to manage the behaviour of pupils in class who may be experiencing social, emotional or behavioural difficulties. If you meet this situation on placement, you can expect that there will be a system in place and general procedures for handling incidents that might arise. You should follow these, taking advice from the teacher. Experience has been rapidly building in this area and effective practical approaches are being shared in teacher's magazines, journals and on websites.

There is also evidence now of some increase in general rowdiness in classes and this can test all teachers. Undoubtedly some schools have an ethos and systems in place which enable them to deal with potentially difficult behaviour much more successfully than other schools; the importance of learning to work within school policies while on placement needs to be emphasised. All teachers need a hierarchy of sanctions to support their discipline strategies and most schools also have positive systems of rewards for exemplary behaviour. For the new teacher there exists a wide range of practical advice on handling confrontations, recognising when you might require assistance, and dealing with worst-case scenarios (for example, Rogers 2002; Roffey 2004).

7 INTERACTION SKILLS AND LEARNING STYLES

QUESTIONING AND EXPLAINING

Ask experienced teachers what is the most important skill in teaching and many will immediately answer 'questioning'. There are several reasons for this. Questioning is regarded as a modern, progressive approach to teaching, involving pupils in an active way. In addition, probing questions are thought to help pupils think deeply and to provide a good check on their understanding. They can also prove a useful management technique: asking a sharp question to someone misbehaving or not attending has a long history as a means of regaining control. So how do you become a skilled questioner in the classroom?

To answer this, it is important first to be clear about the purpose of questioning and its place in the range of teaching techniques. And it may help here to move back a step, in fact as far back as Socrates, in 350 BC. Socrates was renowned as a master questioner and gave his name to the Socratic method, a method of teaching by questioning. Plato describes (in the *Meno*) how Socrates showed, by well-directed questions, that a simple slave boy could demonstrate Pythagoras' famous theorem about the square on the hypotenuse. Following Socrates' example, teaching by questioning developed a long and notable history. As schooling developed, it typically involved pupils learning set knowledge from a textbook and teachers naturally used questioning to test such knowledge. This, together with the influence of the Socratic example, meant that questioning, along with direct exposition, became ingrained in schools and classrooms across the world in a teaching process into which assessment (through oral questioning) was closely integrated. By skilful questioning, teachers sought to elicit ideas dormant in their pupils, to encourage them to think for themselves, and to check their acquisition of set knowledge.

In the 1960s, teaching by questioning came to be considered a distinct improvement on direct exposition, which, it was said, made pupils passive learners. Moreover, it was recognised that young children could not maintain attention for long periods. Questioning kept them active and alert and supposedly helped them to think. You may well remember this as the main way you were yourself taught in school. Questioning came to be seen as the best way to interact in a classroom. The only obvious alternative, direct telling, was increasingly rejected as mere transmission teaching involving passive learning. Some books even championed using a series of questions to structure and convey an explanation. Questioning will certainly figure prominently in your placement schools and, given no other guidance, it is likely to be this approach you naturally adopt in preparing and teaching lessons. After all, what other effective way is there?

Recently, however, there has been increasing recognition that teaching by questioning needs to be looked at much more critically, and that in direct teaching there should be a balance between explaining and questioning. This balance can be found in modern 'direct whole-class interactive teaching' which combines structured explaining with assertive questioning.

Another problem for teaching by questioning has emerged from studies by language experts and sociologists of the typical reality of questioning interchanges in classrooms. The evidence is that most questioning sessions (even so called classroom discussions) are a series of exchanges with the following unremitting form:

Teacher asks question.

Pupil responds.

Teacher asks another question (sometimes with a brief comment on the previous answer – praise, expansion or modification).

One problem with this is that it is more like an interrogation than a conversation or a discussion. Another is that the line of thinking is dominated by the teacher. Pupils basically try to guess the answer the teacher is looking for. Yet another problem is that teachers generally find it hard to ask questions which genuinely probe thinking. It is easier to ask simple recall questions with set answers. In this approach there is little scope for the sustained shared thinking which so many espouse as the aim of their so called discussions based on questioning. In such an interaction process, teachers find it very difficult to handle unexpected answers, contributions or questions from pupils – because these distract from the line of teaching prepared by the teacher. Frankly, they are a nuisance and teachers tend to side-step them with 'We can discuss that later' (they rarely do). Little wonder pupils soon learn not to ask their own questions. Using this approach some teachers do manage to provide stimulating, probing teaching and participative learning; but all too often it results in poor explanation, weak assessment and minimal pupil engagement.

In textbooks on teaching you can find various ways of classifying questions. In practice, however, they boil down to three main distinctions. First, there is the difference between closed and open questions. Closed questions are ones with a right answer, for instance, 'How many legs does a spider have?' The teacher knows the answer and is checking if pupils know it. Most, but not all, closed questions are simple. Some, though, require pupils to work through the logic of a situation and apply an idea to a new context. The basic point, however, is that in a closed question there is a right answer.

Open questions have no single right answer. There may be several good answers (for example, 'How could we test if this material is waterproof?') or the issue might be one where people disagree ('Should fishing be banned?'), or you may be just asking pupils to offer their perspective ('What kinds of novels do you like?'). With this type of question you are trying to get pupils to think for themselves, or apply logic and ideas to what are usually more open problems than in the case of closed questions. Moreover, you respond to pupil answers in a way that develops or challenges their thinking as indicated in their response. It is this kind of question that is expected to develop thinking, and test understanding and abilities. Hence texts on teaching skills encourage teachers to ask more open questions and fewer closed, simple ones.

A second distinction is between simple recall and higher level questions. Recall questions are simple closed ones like asking pupils to name the capital of Australia or the hero in a novel, or to give simple definitions. Higher level questions are ones that require more complex thinking. Many, but not all, of these will be open questions.

A third distinction is between different kinds of higher level question. One famous classification of elements of learning, Bloom's taxonomy (Bloom 1956 and 1964), suggests teachers can ask a range of question types, from simple recall through basic understanding and application, to higher level ones involving analysis, evaluation or synthesis. Other writers point out further differences among higher level questions. Philosophers of education have emphasised a distinction between factual, value, and conceptual questions, each requiring a different approach to finding an answer (respectively, factual evidence, justification of value stances, clarification of meaning, appropriate distinctions and usage). English tutors emphasise how helpful it is in discussing a children's novel to be aware of, for example, questions of deduction ('Why was the farmer angry?'), of imaginative speculation ('What would you do in that context?') and of evaluation ('Was it fair to keep the money?').

To use questioning to develop sustained thinking and test understanding, you need to know the range of question types and be able to generate them in relation to your teaching content. The hard fact of classroom life, however, is that there is massive evidence from studies of questioning that teachers spend most of their time asking low level recall questions. They ask few open or higher order ones. It may now be helpful, in order to find a way forward, to consider the role of questioning in the different modes of teaching discussed in Chapter 2. You will see that this varies considerably from mode to mode.

Direct teaching

In contexts of direct teaching, simple recall questions seem to work well because they give the appearance of participation, thinking and involvement and enable the teacher to move the lesson along a predetermined path. If a teacher asks more complex or open questions, control of the flow and direction of teaching can easily be lost. Hence a step towards using higher order questions might be to separate the explaining from testing phases of direct teaching. The idea would be to base focused explanations on direct telling, not questioning, and to reserve questions for deep probing, using a balance of closed and open questions. Alternatively, a clear exposition might be followed by a genuine discussion of some open issue.

If, however, you do decide to use questioning to structure direct teaching, the following guidelines will help to make it more effective. Focus on a line of thought. Allow some digression but beware of encouraging silly answers or being distracted by pupils. One useful approach is to start with (just a few) low level recall questions to warm up the class and give confidence before moving up to more penetrating questioning. This can work well so long as you signal that you are moving up a gradient and don't remain in the shallows, as so often happens. Another approach is to move in an indirect route towards your central questions, gradually building up a picture of issues and factors (see Wragg and Brown 2001a).

Many successful pupils enjoy being questioned and providing answers, and it gives them further confidence as learners. But for others it is an unenjoyable, even stressful experience, leading to feelings of failure and disaffection from school. Many teachers shy away from explaining that answers are wrong, afraid to de-motivate learners, but it is usually clear to the pupil from the teacher's demeanour that the answer is not what was wanted. Another problem is that it is uncertain how far successful pupils are learning to think by answering questions as opposed to just demonstrating what they already know. For direct teaching, Dillon (1988) suggests teachers focus on preparing a few penetrating questions rather than generating a rash of questions during the lesson. He also urges teachers to ask them 'nice and slow' and to genuinely listen to the answers. Other texts emphasise the importance of effective prompting, expansion and probing of answers so that understanding is fully tested and careful thinking encouraged.

Enquiry

Questioning has a clear role here but it is the learners who should be asking questions. The teacher should model how to formulate questions about the focus of research, for example about the behaviour of the snails being observed by the class or the copy of the historical document being studied. Yet research shows pupils ask very few questions in class – about ten per week compared to the typical teacher's 1,000 per week. Dillon argues that the only way to progress here is to make deliberate room for pupil questions by stopping asking questions yourself and adopting a pedagogy that encourages pupil questions. This involves formally inviting questions, waiting patiently (with an attitude of 'contented expectancy'), welcoming questions when they come and 'sustaining the asking' (because first expressions of a question are rarely the best form; pupils need help to express questions effectively). Eventually you will get a flood of questions and have another kind of problem. This is not really a problem, however, but the first stage of any good research – sorting out a range of possible questions into different types, reducing them where there are overlaps, ranking the questions in terms of importance or interest, and deciding how to find answers to them one at a time.

Discussion

Dillon argues strongly for a tactical avoidance of questions in leading a discussion. This is the reverse of standard practice which assumes that to lead discussion you need to be an excellent questioner. His contention is that teacher questioning foils genuine discussion, turning it into a question-and-answer session which is really part of the direct teaching mode, not genuine open discussion.

But if as a teacher you are not to ask questions how else can you lead a discussion? Dillon offers a list of alternatives to questioning. First are statements. You can just offer your own view, or repeat what a pupil has just said (Pupil: 'It's a cube.' Teacher: 'It's a cube.' Pupil: 'Oh no, it's a cuboid.'), note the contrast between two pupils' contributions ('John said X but Mary is saying Y') or just express your feelings about the situation ('I'm now confused'). Dillon's research evidence shows, to the surprise of most teachers and teacher trainers, that pupils respond in greater depth and length to teacher statements than to teacher questions. In addition to statements, you can use non-verbal gestures (such as passing the turn from one pupil to another with an open hand movement or eye contact), fillers such as 'uhuh' and 'hmm', and expressions of feeling such as 'wow!' or 'nice!' Lastly, there is silence – not a sullen awkward silence but a deliberate, appreciative one of three to five seconds, giving pupils time to think (teachers typically wait less than a second before asking another question if they get no response).

You also need to think out a way to get a discussion up and running without questioning because otherwise you will find yourself quickly resorting to questioning. It will become question and answer and the interaction will be all teacher to pupil and pupil to teacher, not pupil to pupil. A strategy to prevent this is to simply instruct someone to start by offering a view and then instruct another pupil to respond, and so on. Don't join in until this pupil–pupil–pupil pattern is well established and then use Dillon's alternatives for your own contributions. Avoid asking questions. All this depends of course on having a topic that is genuinely open for discussion. Most discussions in classrooms are really question and answer sessions designed to establish or reinforce key points before pupils engage in other activities. But why not just explain these points directly and check understanding, leaving discussion for issues that are properly open to debate?

Action learning

The role of questioning depends to some extent on how open the learning is. Highly structured approaches will lead to practices much as in direct teaching. More open action learning will benefit more from a genuine conversation or discussion style where alternatives to questioning will be more useful. Overall, however, questioning should not play a large role in this mode.

Explaining

In addition to what has been discussed under direct teaching, it is worth noting that Wragg and Brown (2001b) neatly define explaining as giving understanding to a learner. They also helpfully distinguish three main types of explanations: interpretive (which explain meanings of ideas and concepts), descriptive (which explain mechanisms, structures and processes) and reason-giving (which explain causes and effects). Factors in effective explaining include clarity of language, use of motivating, memorable and meaningful examples, and pacing so that learners can take ideas in.

To sum up this half of the chapter, a balance needs to be maintained between explaining and questioning and teachers need to remember that questioning is only one possible way to interact in the classroom. It is misguided to expect just one linguistic form to bear the whole weight of teaching interactions. An advantage of the modes of teaching theory is that it shows clearly where teacher questioning is and is not helpful.

LEARNING STYLES

You will hear a good deal of talk in university classes and in schools about learning styles. There is undoubtedly something important for teachers to understand here. Yet there is also some rather loose talk and confusion about what facts have been firmly established. To try to make sense of this area, it will be important to strive for clarity about basic ideas and theories, to consider carefully what research has so far been able to confirm and, finally, to look at the apparent implications for classroom teaching.

Consider first the idea of style. We can think of a style as a habitual pattern of behaviour or as a preferred way of approaching a task. Take for example a Monty Python 'silly walk' or the way in which you organise your notes (some like to pile everything into one big folder while others are constantly subdividing into sections). On a car journey a passenger doing the navigating may prefer to hold the map upside down – they just find this easier. If someone asks you the way to the post office you may prefer just to use words ('Take the first right then follow the road round till you come to the pub' and so on) or, alternatively, you may feel compelled to start drawing a map on the back of an envelope, or with your finger on a wall. Are styles in this sense in-born, relatively fixed, strong preferences? Or can you easily change your approach to suit circumstances? Research studies do seem to suggest that people have strong, and apparently deep-rooted, preferences in how they approach a learning task or activity. Given a free rein, different people approach the same task in quite different ways, whether it be organising notes, their classroom, making sense of a lecture or reading, or constructing an essay.

Sometimes the term style is used for something one can just turn on when required, as for example in De Bono's concept of 'action shoes' and 'thinking hats' (De Bono 1991, 2000). He uses different kinds of shoes as labels for different styles in approaching a management issue (for instance, pink sneakers are for softly, softly approaches, sensitive to feelings, with purple riding boots for an imperious command style when formal authority needs to be exerted to handle an issue). You might find these 'action shoes' useful in managing a class. Similarly, his 'thinking hats' idea has become popular in several schools (white hat for cool detached thinking, red hat for expressing emotions and so on).

In terms of styles as relatively fixed learning preferences, two well-established differences are between verbalisers and imagers and between holists and analysts. Verbalisers prefer to use words to think and describe. Imagers prefer pictures. Holists like to see the big picture first and work towards a conclusion from there. Analysts like to start with the detail and consider it bit by bit, gradually building up a picture of the whole area. You can often recognise your own style when you find yourself working with someone who is the opposite, say in writing up a report together. Each approach has advantages and disadvantages. Thus holists can miss important detail and jump to conclusions on an overall impression. On the other hand they see the whole wood, not just the trees. Analysts can get bogged down in fragmented detail. More positively, they can build a detailed and eventually well-integrated, comprehensive understanding. An important point to make here is that these particular learning or working preferences appear to be independent of gender, intelligence and personality. You also have to understand that these are just preferences. It is not all black and white. Some have very strong preferences and find it difficult to work in another mode. Others seem to be able to switch more easily as the occasion demands, even though they have a natural preferred style of working.

What different groupings of learning style are there? The problem is that there are many different classifications with different theoretical bases and varying support from reputable research studies. For classroom teaching, the most popular one is known as VAK which stands for visual, auditory and kinaesthetic preferences. Some theorists argue that at root these preferences reflect different ways of processing information and so call them differences in cognitive style. Others use the term learning style. As is common in such research areas, there is a good deal of confusion and overlap in the use of words like style and strategy, learning and cognition. To add to the confusion, some classifications of learning style are based on a supposed combination of personality differences, cognitive processing preferences and other factors. One well known theory (Myers-Briggs 2002) identifies four different personality features whose varied combinations yield sixteen different learning styles. The influential concept of the learning cycle (Kolb 1984) based on four elements (concrete experience, active experimentation, abstract conceptualisation, and reflective observation) has also been used to derive learning style classifications.

Not only is there a large number of competing classifications but the figures different authors produce for the distribution of learning style preferences are highly inconsistent and cast doubt on the accuracy of assessments. Thus one source might claim 90 per cent of the population has a strong visual preference, another that in a typical class about 33 per cent will be auditory, 20 per cent kinaesthetic and 50 per cent visual learners, and yet another that 37 per cent have a kinaesthetic preference. The fact is that there is little hard evidence on the learning styles of young children or how stable their preferences are. Significant differences have been found between the preferences they report and the styles they opt to use when given a choice. Research studies in this area have raised questions of how aware pupils are of learning strategies and how far they can reflect accurately on them. Moreover, it is difficult for researchers and teachers to judge what style is being used at any particular time since many teaching activities often appear to use at least two and sometimes all three – visual, auditory and kinaesthetic. In the case of pupils who claim a kinaesthetic preference, it is not clear that they learn better as opposed to just finding such learning enjoyable. Many girls appear to find kinaesthetic, active approaches helpful for actual learning while boys often find them attractive because they see them as a break from hard learning.

Some teachers claim that taking account of VAK preferences helps them offer more variety in their teaching; but deeper research suggests they barely change their teaching strategies. In some cases they seem merely to have learned new jargon for what they report they have been doing all along to vary their teaching and keep pupils involved.

Educational researchers (for example, Bricheno and Younger 2004; Entwistle and Peterson 2004) have expressed strong concerns about the quality and independence of the evidence base underlying much current commercial and consultancy activity in this area and conclude that it has not yet been demonstrated that there are fixed, stable, differentiated learning styles which can be accurately and easily measured. They point out that much of the less reputable research has involved not studies of learning behaviour but self-report questionnaires where it is all too easy to be self-deluding. Some advocates of VAK and other aspects of learning style cite some research but admit their advocacy is pragmatic rather than research-based (see for example, Bricheno and Younger 2004).

As Entwistle and Peterson (2004) have emphasised, learning style theory is complex and intellectually demanding. It is not easy to develop simple categories or applications or to provide firm research evidence. There is thus a need to suspend judgement in relation to the evidence so far available on learning styles. However, the work on learning styles has at least shown that the cosy assumptions of the past that, say, a predominantly auditory approach will suffice for most classes, just does not hold up. Trying to take account of different learning styles can make teachers interested in individuals as learners, pupils become aware of themselves as learners, and perhaps thus open to new approaches and possibilities which routine or lack of awareness prevented them trying. Teachers and pupils at least now have a language in which to discuss their own learning.

No one now suggests that learners should generally be grouped according to style preferences and taught accordingly (though there may occasionally be a case for this). The idea is rather that in their teaching interactions and design of learning activities teachers should provide, over perhaps a day or week, a range of examples and activities to cater overall for the range of learning styles. To some this may look like a rather raw deal for learners with only a third of a lesson on average matching each style. But two other considerations make this very reasonable. The first is that while individuals may have different style preferences, this does not mean that they can only learn in that style; and, besides, as noted earlier, it is difficult to separate out the different elements of VAK in teaching. Secondly, the range of things to learn and contexts for learning in the modern world make it important for pupils to be able to learn through a range of styles. The teacher's task, as Entwistle (1987) argued, is to help learners become versatile.

A note on teaching style

Many educationists assume teachers unconsciously teach the way they prefer to learn themselves. This seems a reasonable assumption although research confirmation does not appear available. Teaching style might be best described as a preferred overall approach to teaching organisation and interaction. It is important not to confuse an overall style preference in this concept with the various strategies and tactics that might be used in particular circumstances, for example a balance of different modes or management styles using De Bono's ideas discussed above (though in many texts such distinctions are often, unfortunately, blurred). Yet there seems good sense in seeking to develop, within these broad frameworks, an individual style you feel comfortable with.

The main differences in overall style appear between those who favour an informal approach and those who feel much more comfortable with a formal, structured one. No doubt teaching style preferences have links with basic organisational attitudes, but a teacher's style will also probably depend on the models he or she has observed as a pupil or colleague and other factors. The value of observing other teaching is that it can open your eyes to a range of possible ways of teaching well. There is room for variety in teaching and indeed it is important that teachers don't become a group of clones delivering national curricula in a prescribed manner. Part of the deep enjoyment of teaching and basis for developing it is to use your personality fully in communicating learning while being sensitive to differences among your learners.

8 WIDER ROLES AND PROFESSIONAL DEVELOPMENT

At first glance you may think this is a chapter to leave till the end of your course. Surely it is important to focus just now on acquiring confidence and skill as a new classroom teacher, before thinking about wider roles or further development? There are three reasons, however, why you should give attention to this broader picture from the start. First, the standards for qualifying as a new teacher include showing awareness of your wider role and commitment to a process of continuing professional development. These are not extras to be added later. Secondly, the attitudes, skills and qualities of reflective practice are also central to achieving basic classroom competence on your initial training course, helping you to be pro-active in your own learning. Thirdly, you should see yourself as joining the teaching profession the day you start your training, not just think of yourself as a higher education student. This will enhance your confidence and progress.

CONTINUING PROFESSIONAL DEVELOPMENT

Initial training naturally provides a good foundation for a life-long career in the sense that it develops the basic understanding and skills required for teaching. At one time, some teachers tended to act as if on qualifying they were now fully trained for the duration of their career. But significant educational and social changes have put teacher development and school policies into a radically new perspective.

First, the 'knowledge-base' of teaching (and the resources and skills that teachers need to deploy) has changed dramatically with the explosion of ideas about curriculum, learning and teaching. Consider the following, far from comprehensive, list: accelerated learning, brain gym, circle time, the Internet, synthetic phonics, inclusion, formative assessment, critical thinking skills, legislation on disability and discrimination, citizenship education. Many of these developments have their roots in research studies on teaching. In turn, all this has transformed the nature of staff development provision by schools and authorities. And it is inevitable that change will continue apace.

Secondly, the teaching profession has now developed a clear career ladder and taken to heart the need for continuing professional development (cpd for short). The Induction year after graduating has been strengthened to provide further professional development. Thereafter, many possibilities for career development open up as you gain experience and further qualifications. In Scotland (through the Chartered Teacher programme) you can advance significantly in pay and status while remaining a classroom teacher and in the rest of the UK there are various specialist curriculum positions. Moreover, there are teacher networks for curriculum development and practitioner research, often linked to opportunities for advanced qualifications and committed to the idea of reflective practice.

A Scottish report (Deloitte and Touche 2001) argued that, in a profession characterised by continuing innovation, the fundamental idea for the future was 'learning to learn professionally'. It pointed out that no training course can provide a full understanding of, for example, the variety of special needs a teacher might meet. But teachers could grasp a model of how to learn professionally about special needs and other aspects of their role, which they could take forward into their careers. To appreciate how this might be taken forward and what it might involve, it will be useful, first of all, to consider the idea of reflective practice which has long dominated thinking about teacher development.

REFLECTIVE PRACTICE

Teaching can't be learned like a set of recipes for classroom action that will apply to any class or context. There aren't simple answers as to how to manage the behaviour of a disruptive pupil or how to help another pupil grasp the concept of energy or calculus. Contexts vary, learners are unpredictable, you have incomplete information on which to make a decision and yet you have to act. But mere experience is not the answer because some experiences are mis-educative. They ingrain survival skills and bad practice rather than good. Teaching is highly skilled, complex and creative. It requires not just standard techniques (though these do have a role) but intelligent judgement. But professional judgement is a capacity or quality that needs to be learned, just like managing a class or questioning or developing understanding of a subject. It can be developed by reflecting critically and intelligently on experience, in the light of wider ideas and reading, and by adopting a questioning approach to educational practice. You need an ability to evaluate your own professional progress, and a commitment to self-evaluation and to taking charge of your own learning. It also involves becoming aware of the complex relations between theory and practice, recognising that deliberation involves thinking about ends as well as means and value considerations not just practical or technical matters.

As teachers become more expert their actions naturally become more routinised and intuitive. This is progress but there is a danger also that in doing so they can become inward-looking and conservative. Tacit, experience-based knowledge of how classrooms and children work inevitably builds in implicit theories of learning (often involving some defunct theory) and these need to be opened to critical scrutiny from time to time. However, experienced teachers don't constantly reflect. Frankly, they are too busy. It is certainly difficult for teachers to reflect during day-to-day teaching because they have to make quick judgements in the heat of action with little time for conscious reflection. Yet if teaching is to be kept in line with continuing educational change, teachers need time and space to reflect on their teaching approaches and alternative possibilities and to undertake more systematic investigation of their practice.

Teacher development rarely involves straightforward progress. It is more a matter of fits and starts, hitting a plateau and returning to basic ideas. There is a story of a famous golfer who goes to a professional coach every two years and says 'Teach me how to play golf.' He goes back to basics to further improve his already remarkable skills and judgement. Most areas of human expertise are like this and teaching is no exception.

One good way to start reflecting seriously on teaching is to take something that puzzles or interests you. In your early experiences of teaching there will be many issues you find yourself wondering about. Consider, for example, the best way to start a lesson, or bring it to a close or how to give adequate attention to all learners yet cater for particular needs. In reflecting on such issues you should normally adopt a wide perspective, considering not just teaching methods but educational aims and values and examining your beliefs about the nature of knowledge and of how learning works. It will also be helpful to observe closely what actually happens in your current teaching, or ask a colleague to do this. This will enable you to identify positive and negative factors and what other options exist for realising your teaching aims.

Such development through reflective practice as a teacher will often be carried out in a context of top-down governmental, local authority and school initiatives on curriculum and teaching approaches. Teachers need to be aware of these two sources of development, reflective practice and externally led development. While it is hard, at a surface level, for anyone to opt out of externally led development, it has proved much more difficult for such development activities to produce much change in ingrained ways of teaching. New initiatives very quickly tend to become domesticated and assimilated into traditional teaching frameworks and assumptions. Old practices remain with new labels and jargon. Traditional, often unconscious, assumptions (for example about the idea of general ability) and beliefs about educational aims and teaching roles are hard to shift. One good way forward, however, is to take an initiative by beginning some classroom action research, as discussed below.

UNDERTAKING AN ACTION RESEARCH PROJECT

An action research project is basically a project where you select a topic to investigate, try something out in the classroom, monitor its effects, then analyse your results and write up a reflective discussion of your findings. Students in teacher training are often expected to undertake a classroom research project, often carried out as part of a placement later in their course. It is worth orientating yourself to what is involved early on, however, because the basic principles and procedures required can very effectively inform the general development of your teaching.

Students usually find these projects interesting and professionally valuable, provided they avoid some pitfalls and resolve some tensions between being a teacher and researcher – no mean feat because there are two clear tensions: analysis versus action and engagement versus detachment. Teachers generally welcome rational discussion and analysis of educational issues but are constrained by the need to act, to teach 5a on Monday morning or whatever. And in their teaching roles they need to engage fully with their class, which is a very different relationship from the detachment needed for a proper research stance. With careful organisation, however, being a researching teacher is viable, worthwhile and rewarding.

There are various kinds of research project in teacher training courses, including library exercises, case studies, and policy investigations. Advice about these is readily available in a range of general texts for university social science and education students (for example, Bell 1999; Burton and Bartlett 2005).The focus below is on action research projects where you try out a change in teaching with a class or group of pupils.

The main idea to grasp in classroom action research is that of a cycle of planning, acting and reflecting. An action research project can have one main cycle or several shorter cycles leading to a spiral of reflective action (see McNiff 2002). You have to start somewhere and your own choice of topic is a good place to start. Another valuable approach, for example if you are a final year BEd student, is to research some aspect of an area in which your supervisor is currently researching. Here you can benefit from your supervisor's expertise and also contribute, in a small way, to a wider research programme, a useful experience for future professional development.

Two problems arise for action researchers in choosing a topic. One is that many find it hard to focus down to a small enough topic. They think that if the topic is small it is trivial and unimportant. It is as if they want to solve all the nation's educational problems in one fell swoop. But while psychologically this is understandable, in practice you need a topic small enough to get a grip on, given the time and resources available. Focus gives power. Breadth dissipates effort. You need something where your action can make a significant difference. Paradoxically, getting your topic small enough to work on in practice does the opposite of trivialising it. You find you can make progress, gain insights and, instead of remaining narrow, it begins to illuminate many other areas. It may well be something you can profitably share with colleagues who can apply it in their contexts and gradually widen insights and applications.

Another problem is that students often want to reinvent the wheel for themselves in their own classrooms. Take collaborative group work for example. There has been useful research on this, on how it works and what prevents it working well. Yet there is still much to learn. In undertaking an action research project, you need to start from what has already been established. For example, it is already clear that a group of four works well but not more than this, unless it is a discussion. The fact is that groups of seven tend to split up into groups of three and four and even a five has a tendency to split in class. There are six possible interaction paths among a group of four while for a group of seven it is twenty-eight – much more complex. You don't need to discover all this again. It has been well established. But many teachers and students feel compelled to find out for themselves in their classrooms. It would be better, however, to try to see further by standing on the shoulders of previous researchers.

A different problem is the butterfly tendency. Some people beginning action research find it hard to settle on a problem. They opt for a project on questioning but, as they start to explore, they decide the real problem is how children are grouped. Then they conclude the issue is not grouping after all but class discipline. Doubtless as they explore that it will turn out to be something different again. There is a sense in which this is understandable. Problems in classrooms tend to be related. But you have to begin somewhere and really it does not matter where. In the end, what you find about one issue will begin to illuminate others. So, to sum up, focus, don't reinvent the wheel, and don't be a butterfly.

In undertaking your action research project, a first step is to make a reconnaissance. This means scouting out the issue you want to explore, finding out what the problems are in the area you are investigating, getting the lie of the land of your classroom. Observe what happens, what goes wrong and so on. For example, if you are anxious to develop your question-ing, you might record and transcribe a short interchange and see how it differs from what you had hoped would happen. Who does most of the talking? What is the quality of pupil response? Who controls the discussion? Some researchers prefer to do a full reconnaissance and try one well thought out change. Others prefer a series of shorter cycles, making small changes each time as insights emerge and so develop a better practice. Each approach has its strengths. Identifying a pos-sible change can come from thinking on the evidence from your reconnaissance or looking at the literature in the area.

At some stage in a formal research project you need to develop a 'review of the literature' – an analysis of relevant books and articles on the topic. It is best to do as much of this as you can during the process of firming up a topic and planning your research (though timing issues sometime make this difficult) while also being prepared to read and analyse further at the write-up stage. What particular data gathering methods you choose (for example, systematic observation, questionnaires, interviews) will depend very much on what you are researching. For formal projects in BEd or BA courses you can expect guidance on research methods (there is often a module on this) including how to reduce bias, ethical considerations and how to analyse and report your findings effectively. This will enable you to put your planned teaching change into action, sustain it properly, troubleshoot any difficulties and monitor the effects. Then you can analyse the evidence you have gathered and write up your report. Remember, here, that your change does not have to have worked to be useful or to count as a good research project. Experiments and action research studies which fail are often at least as illuminating and eventually contribute as much to improved teaching as those where things go right. The important thing is to reflect intelligently on the evidence and its implications for taking teaching forward.

BUILDING A PROFESSIONAL DEVELOPMENT PORTFOLIO

You need to be organised to take charge of your own professional development. A haphazard, informal approach will make your professional learning just like that – haphazard and informal. No doubt some good things will happen and development strategies do benefit from a spontaneous element, but you will lose focus and power and dissipate effort if you do not adopt an organised approach, and manage your resources and time well. During your training course the best way of doing this is to build up a professional development portfolio, linked to the expected teaching standards but opening out beyond these. You need to think carefully about how a portfolio can help if it is not to become another chore.

In most teacher training contexts now you are expected to develop a portfolio to demonstrate acquired competence and to guide further development. In some cases, student teachers feel they are expected to provide voluminous evidence to confirm achievement of QTS. In others, the emphasis is on promoting professional development not just confirming competence. Often this goes hand in hand with conducting your own formal audit of your development towards the standards. Within this arrangement, the twin pillars for success are a well-organised and intelligently developed portfolio and a clear use of the standards, viewed in critical perspective, as a framework for your development thinking and action planning.

Much portfolio development (and reflections in teaching files) can easily become routine writing without an action focus and an amalgamation of a massive load of documents without any clear organisation, structure or evident usefulness. You need to develop your portfolio in a way which minimises paperwork and prevents mere accumulation of paper. Try to be selective and focused from the start. If you find that your particular context appears to expect you to amass every possible piece of paper as evidence of your development and competence then quickly seek a discussion with your mentor so that a reasonable way forward can be agreed.

The best basis for professional portfolio development is not just the traditional one of reflective practice but 'learning to learn professionally' as discussed above. Effective professional development is not a linear process but an open cycle of development, through action and reflection, in a situation of complexity (Hoban 2002). In other words, teacher development is not a straightforward, top-down, narrow training process but a much messier, open and creative process, drawing on support and ideas from a range of interacting sources. You need to learn how to draw together ideas from these potential different sources of learning: pre-course experiences and conceptions, university studies, placement, ICT resources and networks, individual and collaborative opportunities and networking with recent graduates. You need to internalise a model of developing professional understanding and skills by drawing on these sources in a way that can be applied throughout a career as new policies, priorities and ideas develop.

To adapt an idea from Lave and Wenger (1991), teacher training involves not merely or centrally a 'teaching' curriculum (delivered by ITE or school staff in a traditional manner) but a 'learning' curriculum. This is one which enables students to draw on the community of professionals and the network of learning resources for the profession (in the university, schools and the community at large). It is also worth emphasising again here the interactive trio of understanding and knowledge, skills and abilities, and values and personal commitments which form the basis for teacher training standards. To realise these ideas in portfolio development, it is perhaps better to think in terms of building a 'process folio' (Gardner 1999). A traditional portfolio of finished work typically includes examples of work done, and a record of events, achievements and evaluations. A process folio, as envisaged here, would also include documentation of the process and sources of learning, reflections and action plans. It would be a record which sought to capture the reality of the substance, sources and processes of professional learning. This would serve as a framework and stimulus for further professional enquiry and activity. Whichever approach to portfolio development you use, as far as possible you should develop your folio as an electronic, multimedia folio, supplemented where necessary by hard copy material. This is a very useful way to develop your confidence and skill in using ICT.

WIDER PROFESSIONAL ROLES AND RESPONSIBILITIES

Classroom teaching of subject knowledge and skills is only part of your role as a teacher. You will find you are expected to have a much wider view of your commitments, as the QTS and other standards indicate. You need to become aware of a range of teacher responsibilities – legal, administrative, pastoral and contractual. Placement is a good place to observe these aspects in action, and so consolidate principles and content studied in the university. Issues like child protection and health and safety are of course paramount. Pupils' personal and social development and pastoral care require attention, as does care for the environment. You also need to know about policies regarding special needs, including those of gifted and talented pupils, and inter-agency working (that is liaison with other professionals like social workers and health personnel). Citizenship was introduced as a national curriculum subject in 2003 in England and is a national priority in Scotland. There has been much development work in this area and all teachers are expected to have a role in addressing it in schools. You will be expected as a teacher to communicate effectively with parents and contribute to the corporate life of the school and to school development planning. You are expected to take an interest in educational research and keep up to date with findings in your area, for example by reading teacher-focused summaries and dissemination material and to know about ideas like evidence-based practice.

All this can undoubtedly look daunting. Again, however, teachers and schools do manage. Successful teachers integrate these ideas into their classroom role and regular thinking about curriculum, teaching and assessment, and into their work as a member of a school team.

PARENTS AND TEACHERS

Official educational publications acknowledge parents are the child's first and enduring educators and that they play a crucial role in helping children learn. Family learning initiatives are now recognised as a powerful way for reaching the most disadvantaged in society with the potential to reinforce the role of the family and change attitudes to education, helping to build strong local communities and widening participation in learning. Governments are concerned to help schools develop effective baseline assessment (that is checking on their accomplishments soon after they start school) so that appropriate developmental goals and targets can be set and monitored and children experiencing difficulties identified early and given appropriate support.

Traditional approaches to parental partnership adopted what is now recognised as a patronising attitude. Schools and teachers saw themselves as the ones with the expertise on education with the role of encouraging parents to take an interest in their children's education and to become involved in parents' evenings and fundraising. This approach has been slowly giving way to a deeper recognition of the complementary partnership in education between teachers and parents and the important knowledge of their children as learners that most parents have, although there is still a danger that parents are only seen as an extra pair of hands for the teacher (Slater and Bremner 2003; Edwards and Warin 1999). If you are taking a teacher training course focused on early education you will be expected to learn about parental communication and partnership in depth. A good range of practical advice and guidance exists on effective parental involvement in early years settings both in home and school contexts (for example, Merttens et al. 1996). At later stages of education communication, dialogue and support initiatives have centred on career choices, examination concerns and behavioural issues.

The national curriculum was motivated partly by the aim of improving communication with parents about school performance so that choices could be made, and in terms of parental rights. Recent surveys have found that what parents want is clear communication in language they can understand, approachable rather than defensive attitudes from teachers and a willingness to listen to the parent's point of view and treat their children with respect. They expect a positive approach from schools and consultation at the transition to secondary education and during subject choices.

PART III
Study Skills for Teacher Training

9 APPROACHES TO STUDY

When you are studying do you find yourself just skating along the surface of the text? Or are you determined to try to understand the ideas for yourself, however long it takes? Or do you focus on finding the easiest way to get the highest grades and is that your real goal? Not all students study in the same way. Researchers have found that students in higher education tend to adopt one of these three approaches, labelled surface, deep and strategic (Entwistle 1996). These different approaches to study have been shown to make a big difference to student success and learning.

This chapter begins by explaining these different approaches to study and then applies these ideas to the kinds of study you will encounter in teacher training. First, how to get the most from lectures, tutorials, seminars and workshops is considered. This is followed by a discussion of how to read, critically and constructively, books, articles and research reports on education, and how to make good notes. Lastly, advice is offered on how to prepare for examinations and face them with confidence.

SURFACE, DEEP AND STRATEGIC LEARNING

It is very important to note that the various approaches to study do not pinpoint inherent qualities in students. No one is by nature a surface learner, for example. These are approaches students adopt for various reasons to suit particular circumstances.

Surface

You will be tempted to adopt a surface approach to learning when you

- are not really motivated or engaged by the subject;
- are aiming only for a bare pass with minimal work;
- find the work difficult;
- do not have enough time to study and get in a panic;
- believe that success depends on a good memory for mugging up facts, irrespective of understanding.

In such circumstances you can find yourself reading and rereading your notes hoping something will stick; or writing an essay by merely reproducing what is in the textbooks without getting on top of the ideas and making them your own. You just hope what you have written is sufficiently distinctive to avoid accusations of plagiarism. This will not prove satisfying, either for yourself as a learner or for your tutor. Some contexts encourage surface learning. Traditional examinations are often accused of this, at times unfairly. You focus on the surface facts, don't bother about trying to relate things, don't try to distinguish the wood from the trees. Learning becomes a drag with negative feelings and little enjoyment.

Teacher education assessments, however, increasingly involve performances like presentations, real or simulated teaching, and evaluations of curriculum materials – tasks requiring application of ideas and techniques, not just knowledge reproduction. Students usually regard such tasks as highly relevant and meaningful. Provided you are able to organise your study time effectively, maintain commitment to becoming a good teacher, and have a basic grasp of the ideas you are exploring, you should be able to avoid a surface approach to your studies. Even if a subject is rather new to you, or one you did not do well on before, in embarking on teacher training there is a chance for a fresh start. Whatever the subject matter – be it mathematics, science, psychology, art, and so on – you can learn in a more genuine and effective way by a combination of hard work and sound study techniques, alert to the aims of deep and strategic learning.

Deep

You will tend to adopt a deep approach where you really feel a need to understand things, get inside the topic and become an expert on it. You will focus on transforming your knowledge, constructing your own understanding, linking it to previous ideas and your own network of knowledge, experience and thinking. This is an active meaning-making process, not a memory process. You grasp new concepts which help you make sense of the topic (for example the deficit model of special educational needs or the idea of learned helplessness). Of course, you have to understand the basic ideas of the discipline and its aims and methods, but you also have to build your own unique understanding, viewpoint and way of thinking about it. When you adopt a deep approach, you are likely to find yourself boiling down your notes to a framework you have developed for yourself from reading, so that you can rehearse your own understanding.

You focus on the underlying meaning, the big picture, key themes, principles and concepts, powerful ideas to drive analysis. You also seek effective application examples to develop your expertise in this area – more like a working professional than a student. Yet you can't just rely on the big picture alone; you need the detail to see the big picture and how these details interrelate, but can develop it interactively. Such learning is often highly satisfying, challenging and even exhilarating (see Entwistle and Peterson 2004). As Bruner (1960) pointed out, the key ideas in any subject are powerful but also simple – at least once understood! What leads to clear thinking in a discipline is mastering the basic ideas, internalising them, and learning to apply them to issues and problems. The secret is to make sure you understand the basic ideas in your own terms. Otherwise you may fall into a surface approach.

Strategic

Strategic learners tend to focus on getting clear about exactly what is expected in the assignment or exam, clarifying the criteria for doing well, and then organising their study and working out how to get the highest possible mark. They tend to plan their time well, find out what the lecturer wants and keep disciplined. Deep learners can sometimes, by contrast, give the disciplined organisation of study second place to their determination to pursue understanding for its own sake. But courses have time constraints and assignment deadlines!

The emerging view from research is that approaches to study are neither wholly innate nor wholly determined by context. Students appear to have predilections for one or another approach, but the interaction of these with the context leads to them adopting particular strategies. An approach to study can soon become a habit, however. Hence you need to think out your strategy and take steps to minimize factors which might prevent you adopting the best possible approach. In most teacher training contexts you will probably get on best if you are both deep and strategic. Circumstances in which the most sensible strategy is a surface one should be rare. If you find you are adopting a surface approach you would be well advised to seek support from the student study advice centre. This will help you identify the factors causing this and show you how to change to a more effective and satisfying strategy for your professional learning. If you are too narrowly strategic, however, you may fail to develop the deep understanding which can serve you well throughout your career.

MAKING NOTES FROM LECTURES

There is a difference between making notes (actively deciding what to write down) and passively taking notes (trying to capture everything the lecturer says). The reality of lectures and study patterns, however, makes it difficult to make rather than take notes in lectures, whatever books on how to study advise. Some compromise is necessary, matched to the particular lecture context.

In universities today you will find a range of lecturing styles. Traditional exposition may be supplemented by a handout. Some will use PowerPoint presentations with detailed information on a sequence of slides. These may be put on an e-mail conference for you before or after the lecture so that you can download them or given as a handout in the lecture, perhaps with spaces in which you can write further notes. If there is no handout, you will certainly want to make good notes during the lecture. If a full handout or an electronic version is made available, you may be tempted not to make more notes. Don't succumb. The best approach is always going to be to work hard during the lecture in a disciplined way rather than to sit back and have to do the hard work later on. If you already have a handout or a promised electronic copy just make your own additional notes as you listen. Intelligent note making is a discipline which will help you to understand and pay attention and develop a reasonable grasp of the ideas.

Students do find it difficult, however, to write notes and reflect on what is being said at the same time. One answer is to use a mixture of techniques. First of all, you need to develop your own short cuts in writing – 'ed' for education, 'ass' for assessment, and so on. You will save much time with clear shorthand and legible writing. It is amazing how often some students needlessly write out in full. Overcome any inhibitions here and use shorthand, without becoming cryptic. Secondly, remember you don't have to take down every word the lecturer says, merely the key points and examples. If you are actively thinking as you write this will be easier than if you merely write down everything. In a lecture on assessment you might note:

Summative – to measure L (check what I'd)

Formative – to improve L thru feedback. Diff is aim not type/timing of ass.

L here is short for learning, diff for difference, ass for assessment. The lecturer might actually have said: 'There is an important distinction between formative and summative assessment. The basic distinction is one of aim. Summative sums up attainments, it measures learning to check how much and how well the pupils have learned . . .' and much more.

You need to realise that lectures don't just convey information but try to enthuse and motivate further study and exploration, provide an overview framework of concepts and theories, and exemplify the kind of thinking involved in problem-solving in the area. In a good lecture you will see a mind actively at work in the discipline concerned and will pick up emphases and nuances hard to convey in handouts. You may get a chance to ask questions. You may find it useful to make a concept or knowledge map (a linked diagram of key points) of the area as a way of capturing the ideas in the lecture. Some, however, find this does not suit them, despite the exhortations of those who do. You will never know, however, until you give it a sustained trial. In lectures, where style and content vary so much, you will constantly have to balance actively reflecting and making notes and just taking down things you may otherwise miss.

Afterwards, you should organise your notes in whatever way suits you, clarifying the key points. Follow up any issues on which you are not clear with other students or the tutor. Plan a space for this shortly after the lecture and keep this discipline. The effort will repay you handsomely and save time in the long run.

E-LEARNING

E-learning is used here as a term to cover all the learning involving information and communications technology (ICT), such as computers, e-mail, the Internet, CD-ROMs and various multimedia resources you will find yourself using over your course. Such e-learning is an increasingly significant feature of teacher education, as of higher education generally.

It is important that you develop your skills and confidence here because it will be a key aspect of your teaching role to help pupils use ICT in their learning, as well as exploiting it in your teaching.

To be successful as an e-learner you need to take account of some key differences between e-learning and more traditional forms of study. First, it puts a premium on building confidence as an independent learner, learning to plan and manage your own learning, being able to assess yourself carefully and taking responsibility. You will of course need to continue to build up your computer skills. In e-learning you will have more control of the time, place and also pace of your study, a vast range of resources via the world wide web, and access to multimedia working. This is why self-confidence and responsibility need to go hand in hand. In searching and browsing resources you need discipline, a clear sense of priorities and of effective time use.

Browsing, e-mail conferencing and networking with fellow students are all important. For example, sharing ideas for teaching, asking questions from your tutors and fellow students, and finding lesson plan ideas on the web can help enormously and save precious time. Moreover, your tutor can target you directly with a personalised response to your need if you learn to pinpoint your query. Don't, however, expect a constant stream of communication from your tutor and write concise not verbose e-mails. While you do need some space for open-ended browsing, overall you should be disciplined, focused and maintain a certain ruthlessness, or you will fritter away time.

Reading and note-making skills in e-learning will emphasise searching, browsing, skimming and awareness of the nature of web pages with their links to related concepts as opposed to the linear, page after page form of textbooks on your library shelves. Quality control can be a big problem. Check date, author, academic status and links to more robust studies and reputable references. On learning styles, for example, there are some sound academic references along with a great deal, frankly, of dross and hype. You need to learn to distinguish these categories.

UNIVERSITY CLASSES

In your programme you are likely to have some mixture of tutorials, curriculum classes or workshops, and perhaps also some seminars and individual consultations before a placement. Terms vary and a seminar in one institution may be called a tutorial or even workshop in another. Tutorials are usually linked to lectures and aim to help you understand and apply to practical cases the ideas in the lecture. Seminars tend to be more discursive and may involve one student reading a short paper or making a brief presentation each week. Workshops typically have an active, practical flavour (for example in arts, mathematics, and sciences). In teaching methods classes the activity might involve planning a set of lessons or a unit of work. In many courses you will have a formal individual consultation with your tutor before a placement. This can be helpful in discussing your professional development aims and needs, clarifying aspects of the placement guidelines and getting to know the tutor who will be visiting you. Such meetings can work well if you are proactive in suggesting what you'd like to discuss and think out a few professional development targets relating to the standards.

All these types of class or contact can vary in quality depending on the tutor and on your own preparation and engagement. If you are coming straight from school, you will find much less spoon-feeding and more expectation of initiative and self-organisation. If you are on a postgraduate route, you will already have a range of experiences of tutorials and seminars and be alert to what makes them work well or badly. Tutorials can easily turn into mini-lectures by the tutor if students don't ask questions or participate. Seminars can reduce to only surface level learning for students other than the presenter. Effectively managed ones, however, will enable you as a speaker to rehearse your understanding of ideas and issues and, as a member of the audience, to learn to think critically, challenge and probe. Try to prepare for tutorials and see them as contexts for learning how to clarify and apply ideas to particular cases, consider evidence for theories and viewpoints, understand difficult readings and so on.

Workshops can vary in quality. Well-designed problem-solving activities on curriculum planning or case studies of children with learning difficulties can combine independent group working, consultation and plenary review. Problem-based learning (where small groups work actively to research and resolve an issue) is increasingly being used in teacher education. When supported by lectures, this can mean real engagement in relevant learning activities. So can modelling exercises like teaching reading, science or technology. Some curriculum workshops will be part lecture or class teaching and part hands-on activities like planning lessons, preparing teaching materials and simulated teaching. In so far as they tend to direct teaching the advice on making lecture notes applies. In so far as they involve genuine discussion and more active student roles you should involve yourself fully, not being afraid to ask questions or expose ideas for scrutiny. They generally provide a non-threatening environment where you can make mistakes as you gradually clarify ideas and develop practical skills and useful teaching ideas and strategies.

Some classes provide a stream of practical ideas and hand-outs. This can appear overwhelming but the point is to store them away for future use. You will find this range of teaching ideas stimulates your imagination and gives you confidence that you can quickly devise something in a given situation as you begin a placement.

Tutorials, seminars and workshops enable you to get to know fellow students well and to develop friendships and support networks. Many find these carry into their early careers. You should also actively use student representatives to suggest to tutors, or the course director, ways in which these classes could be improved.

READING

There are many different kinds of books and articles to study during teacher training. You need to be aware of the different kinds and what you can expect to get out of them. There will be books and articles on psychology, sociology, philosophy of education, official reports, research papers, practical texts, teacher guides and so on. The Internet will have a range of offerings of varied usefulness. Try gradually to get a feel for what each kind can offer and how best to use them to develop your ideas, skills and understanding. You should have little difficulty in remembering, absorbing and noting ideas from practical texts and teacher guides, but maintain a critical eye in considering practical tips.

Modern official reports are much more reader-friendly than formerly. You will want to have a clear understanding of policies and professional expectations. There may be details you are expected to be thoroughly familiar with and, after preliminary study, such familiarity is best developed through sustained experience in using the documents in planning teaching in workshops and on placement. Look critically, however, at their rhetoric and practical implications and underlying assumptions about teaching and learning. With more difficult theory and research articles, focus on the bits that are readily understandable, learn to live with some difficult passages and fight through the jargon and any abstract or bureaucratic writing. You can't expect to understand everything at once. Such texts are generally written for academic peers rather than specifically for prospective teachers; but they may be the only source of some important evidence and arguments. With research studies, there is often a summary of basic findings in ordinary accessible language. Some research publications are now deliberately aimed at teachers.

To understand an issue or topic (for example child development) you will typically need to study more than one source; but don't try to read through ten such texts. For all texts, try to grasp the author's perspective sympathetically as well as looking closely at evidence claims, the logic of argument and its assumptions and values. Give a text a chance to convey its message and perspective. This will help you appreciate alternative views. Your reading should be critical as well as appreciative. Critical need not mean destructive criticism. It can involve appraising the strengths as well as weaknesses of a view or book. Consider what confidence can be placed on factual claims and arguments, be alert to special pleading and the logic of supposed practical implications. Look closely at their basic assumptions and perspectives about aims, values, and teaching.

One approach to effective reading is known as SQ3R. It looks formulaic but using its simple principles can provide a secure platform for developing a more flexible approach. Basically you first survey (skim) the text to develop a quick overview. Then you develop questions you will look for answers to in the text. Then you read closely to find answers, rehearse these and finally review what you have learned. Make notes as needed. Your questions might come from ideas about a forthcoming essay or exam. A useful strategy would be to internalise such an approach and then adapt it to the messy reality of reading and thinking about educational ideas.

Sometimes students assume that a modern text for students is bound to be clearer and more helpful than an original text or research report. This is not at all necessarily so. Classic educational writings, for instance by Plato, Aristotle, Rousseau, Matthew Arnold and Dewey, are worth reading for themselves. Their examples may be old fashioned and you need certainly to translate them to fit the modern classroom. But the core ideas and arguments are often expressed with force and style and there is a chance to appreciate sharp educational minds at work. Bruner's *The Process of Education* (1960) and Stenhouse's *An Introduction to Curriculum Research and Development* (1975) are still worth reading and available in university libraries.

HOW TO SUCCEED IN EXAMS

Many teacher educators frown on examinations as an unsuitable way of assessing students on teacher education programmes. Exams, they say, encourage memorisation rather than understanding, surface rather than deep learning and separate theory from practice. Steps can be taken, however, by staff and students to surmount these dangers; and exams are still used in a limited way in many teacher education courses, contributing a proportion (say 40 per cent) of the marks for a module, with the rest coming from an essay, presentation or assignment. This is because exams retain academic status as a traditional, hard test of learning, and because universities are concerned about plagiarism. Many academics see exams as the main way of checking that students can answer, unaided and in their own voice, questions designed to probe their understanding of the subjects they have been studying.

In teacher education, many examinations consist of essay questions. You might, for example, be expected to write three essays in a two-hour examination. There are also multiple choice exams (some courses have these for mathematics and religious education), open book examinations (you can bring in key texts – which discourages memorisation tactics), short answer formats (which test basic understanding and coverage) and indeed the whole range of modern examination varieties.

All students can improve examination technique, and the way they approach exam preparation has been shown to make a big difference to grades and success rates. A first step is to develop a positive attitude and clear, realistic view of how exams work and how examiners operate. There are several common myths and rumours about exams that need to be dispelled. It is not cynical to see exams as a kind of academic game with rules you need to understand and play to. Much occupational life has game-like features. Being strategic as a student and learner and using some simple techniques can help you succeed. In the examination game, the factors that help most are a confident and a positive attitude, strategic thinking, technique, and a pro-active approach. If you are someone who really gets worked up about exams, your university will have a study advice centre where staff will address your particular needs.

You should know, first, that examiners are not out to trick you and exams are not intended as memory tests or speed writing tests. You are expected to demonstrate adequate knowledge and understanding using normal memory powers and writing speeds. Far from looking for ways to fail you, examiners are in fact keen to reward knowledge and try to be fair so long as you follow the instructions properly, answer the question asked and try to meet the criteria. Examiners are commonly given marking schemes which explain where they should give marks. Hence their mind set is to look for content in your script to award marks. Essays will normally be judged in terms of a few criteria (such as well argued and evidenced, showing understanding of key ideas and awareness of alternative views). You should have access to these criteria so that you can prepare with these in mind.

What then tends to go wrong? This can be summed up as follows: poor understanding as a result of surface learning; not reading the question; poor timing; irrelevant content, waffle not facts or analysis; too few clear, concise examples (or overlong ones) to illustrate your understanding; failure to apply key ideas; poor notes, exam planning and revision; poor essay writing technique. The solution is to take charge of your own preparation for examinations and develop a positive attitude. Aim to develop confidence in your own knowledge and ability to demonstrate it under test conditions. Be pro-active in finding out the structure and nature of the forthcoming exam; don't wait for tutors to tell you or spoon-feed you. Build into your study short periods of time for relaxing and maintain your health through a good diet, exercise and sleep. Some students find self-help groups a boon while others work better independently. Whatever your preference beware rumour mongers and panic merchants.

Begin exam preparation early, having checked the aims and content of the exam, collect materials, books, and examples of past papers. Organise your notes to avoid a last minute rush to the library only to find all copies of key texts are out. The struggle should be in the preparation; sitting the exam should be the easy bit!

The very best advice is to do past papers. You need to understand why this works so well, however, or you are likely to neglect it. It gives experience of the process of applying ideas and examples to potential questions. Don't be put off by the thought that this particular question is unlikely to be repeated in your exam. You are gaining experience of a process which will help you to apply relevant particular, detailed knowledge and understanding to whatever question comes up.

Don't try to work up a prepared, memorised full answer to a question you've spotted. Exams are not memory tests or guessing games. Memorised answers tend to contain much that is irrelevant to the question, which is rarely quite the same as you predicted. A better approach is to show examiners you can develop an argument in answer to a question on the basis of good general understanding, an ability to apply ideas and a sufficient command of detail and examples to illustrate the ideas. Hence, plan your answer during the exam, drawing on intelligent preparation not speculative memorisation.

Revision should not be last minute. A better strategy is to plan active revision as you work through the course. Remember you can't read everything or reproduce everything in the exam. You will only have space for so many examples and details. Aim for active rereading of lecture notes, map key ideas and organise your knowledge into potential arguments. Revision need not be reading over notes or writing things out. Think about what learning style suits you. Some prefer to speak ideas out loud, others to draw diagrams, concept maps, others to be even more active physically. Multiple ways will help reinforce things whatever your revision preference.

Educational exams require good arguments, evidence and understanding and ability to use knowledge, not just to reproduce it. You need to provide detail but not overkill or you will not have a good structure or make your points effectively.

Make it easy for the examiner to give you a good mark. Use examples to show you understand the key ideas you use in your discussion. You need to show evidence of having understood the basic concepts of the course and of having read more widely than just your lecture notes and one text. Memorised quotations aren't expected. Instead explain key ideas in your own words, acknowledging experts' ideas simply, without formal references (for example, 'Bruner's theory of scaffolding is that . . .').

Aim to show the examiner you can write relevantly and coherently, adopt a questioning approach and use evidence and argument well. Look over the advice on writing essays in Chapter 10 and adapt to an examination context. Look for words like describe, analyse, compare, discuss, list, evaluate. For short answer questions, you need to be clear about exactly what is asked for and provide it clearly and concisely. For multiple choice items, a good strategy is to answer the ones you are sure of at a steady pace, then work carefully at the rest, eliminating obviously wrong options before making your final, best judgement.

On the day it will be natural to experience some tension. This actually aids performance. If you have prepared effectively there is no reason to worry. You can have confidence that you are on the right lines and are doing your best. Replace any negative thoughts with positive ones. Don't be put off by rumours or others' panic. After taking a minute to say hello and wish your friends well, you may find it best to keep to yourself just before the exam so you can focus and build up your determination to do well.

During the exam you need to manage your time in a serious, disciplined way. This can prove a big factor in your success. Failure to attend to this point can lead to lower grades than your revision effort and basic knowledge suggest you are capable of. Many find it helpful to do the question they are most confident about first. Remember, also, you tend to get most marks from the early sections of your exam answers. Keep some check on the wording of the question and that you are writing relevantly as you go.

Leave enough time to think about the question and make an outline plan before you start writing. This will save thinking time while writing and your writing will be more structured and flow better. Five to seven minutes of planning for a one-hour essay can pay rich dividends. Monitor yourself and keep to time for each question. Breaking up an answer into sections can help to keep you clear and focused. Write at a good pace but ensure it is legible and finish the paper, answering all the questions expected. If pressed for time for your last question, a bare outline of ideas may show enough core understanding to gain a pass.

Leave enough time to read through your script when you have finished. After the exam get on with other things, including doing some leisure activity you enjoy. Avoid a post mortem until you know the result. You may get a pleasant surprise. If you do not do as well as you hoped, determine to learn from the experience. Finally, keep a sense of proportion. There's a lot more to life and teacher training than exams.

10 WRITING ESSAYS

ESSAYS AND PROFESSIONAL LEARNING

Whatever route into teacher training you take, you will have to write some essays or assignments. Some students welcome this, having done well in essays in their previous studies. Others haven't had such rewarding experiences. For everyone, one key to success is to realise that researching and writing essays and assignments is one of the best ways to learn in depth about education and teaching; they are not just a vehicle for assessing knowledge and understanding.

Studying education is not a matter of mugging up set knowledge or parroting official policies. Policies and practice are hotly debated, and thinking, policy development and research studies continue to bring new insights. Hence teachers need a good grasp of educational ideas and also the ability to think and argue effectively about educational issues and practices. Both these aspects figure prominently in the aims of most teacher education courses across the UK. Here, for example, are expectations from the Scottish benchmark statements (Quality Assurance Agency for Higher Education 2000):

Acquire a broad and critical understanding of the principal features of the education system, educational policy and practice.

Draw on relevant principles, perspectives and theories to inform professional values and practices.

Acquire an understanding of research and its contribution to education.

Access and evaluate professionally relevant literature.

Construct and sustain reasoned and coherent arguments about educational matters and professional practices.

At a more detailed level they specify that students should know how to:

- search for relevant literature;
- analyse, interrogate and evaluate educational writings;
- develop sound arguments;
- construct effective reports on educational matters.

Undertaking written assignments is crucial to developing all these qualities. Furthermore, assignments often draw directly on work undertaken on school placements. Hence they help you learn how to link theoretical understanding to classroom practice. Essays should also help you develop your own writing skills. This is important since teaching effective written communication (good writing as well as correct English) is an important classroom role in primary schools, for secondary English and indeed all teachers ('every teacher is a teacher of English').

Undergraduate students entering teacher training who studied science subjects rather than English and history may feel less confident about writing educational essays. Likewise for postgraduate courses a science graduate may not have written an essay since leaving school and a mature student may not have written one for twenty years. Teacher education faces the challenging task of responding to the increasing diversity of its learners and helping all achieve high standards in writing about education. Everyone needs to start from where they are. All will have some strengths to exploit (based on their academic, employment and life experiences), almost everyone will be writing assignments specifically on education for the first time; and anyway writing about education is different from writing essays in English or history.

Real progress can be made given clear guidance and constructive feedback. And, like so much else, writing effectively about education is a matter of continuing development as contexts for deploying writing skills emerge throughout a career, such as written communication with parents and advanced professional studies.

Experience suggests that you are likely to write good educational essays and assignments if you

- are clear about the aims and purposes of different kinds of essay or assignment;
- work at understanding the criteria for marking the assignment;
- aim for a deep understanding of the subject matter of the essay;
- think how best to research and construct each particular essay taking account of your preferred working style;
- work at constructing a clear and effective discussion of the issues;
- remain alert to expectations regarding style, tone, presentation;
- apply your best writing skills in developing your script.

All these aspects are discussed here.

DIFFERENT TYPES OF EDUCATIONAL ESSAYS

In your course you are likely to meet different kinds of essay or assignment. Some assignments are more like analytical reports than creative essays or an examination of one text in depth. Consider, for example, an essay on children's development and learning, a shadow study of a secondary school pupil, or a case study of a child experiencing a difficulty in learning. As reports, however, they are not the same as typical business or laboratory reports, based on bullet points and short factual sections covering different aspects. They are something in between.

Suppose a child development assignment asks you to observe children in your class, then report and analyse your observations in relation to research and theory of child development. This means analysing in the sense of looking for what variations and patterns emerge and explaining your findings by drawing on ideas and research evidence from books and articles. You might begin by outlining some key ideas (for example, 'stage of development', 'constructivism') that will guide your analysis. Overall, the assignment demands concise and accurate reporting with an eye to relevance of contextual detail, quality of evidence and an ability to relate your observations to your growing, critical understanding of theory and research findings. If you are also asked to consider implications for teaching, you will need to broaden your reading to cover modern ideas on teaching strategies and then apply practical judgement in the light of your analysis and awareness of the context.

In contrast, consider an essay that asks you to find relevant sources and build your own response to the question 'What makes for good teaching?' This is an invitation to develop and defend a personal stance with arguments and evidence. It is certainly a topic on which every intending teacher can be expected to have a view. Since it is very wide you will have first to narrow it down, perhaps focusing on a few teaching aims and how to achieve them, or restricting yourself to three features of 'good teaching'. You may face two temptations, both of which need to be strongly resisted. One is to find what other writers have said and just summarise or briefly paraphrase their ideas, linking them loosely together. This, largely reproduction of existing ideas, is not likely to be worthwhile, impressive or gain a high mark. By all means summarise others' ideas for yourself as short notes as a start to drafting your essay. But then look critically at these ideas and develop your own response. The second temptation is to assume that markers only want 'your opinion' and consequently just trot out a series of ideas from your experience and background, relying heavily on anecdotes, general slogans and educational clichés, supported by a range of authoritative quotations to add respectability. Your tutors, however, are not looking just for your unsupported opinion, a statement of your own educational creed. They require evidence and argument, awareness of what has been said by established educational thinkers about the issue and a reasoned case.

In an open essay on 'good teaching' you would be expected to construct and defend, by close argument and critical evaluation of readings, an argued personal stance on aims and values. The emphasis would be on clear thinking, clarifying the meanings of the main ideas you may be discussing (for example 'child-centred', 'process'), the sense in which you are referring to 'good' (is it in the sense of 'desirable' or merely as 'effective'?) and the values and evidence which inform your arguments (with possibly brief reference to your own experience). You would need to look closely at the logic of your argument. Most people enter teacher training with decided views about what teaching is for and how it should be conducted, based on beliefs about the nature and aims of education they have grown up with. The essay is asking you to draw on these values and assumptions, look critically at them and express and defend your considered views.

In short, neither of the extremes is wanted but something in between. The way to providing it is to look closely at the criteria for marking the essay. You have a right to expect these to be set out along with the essay topic. If not, you should ask for them. It is good practice in assessment to share the criteria for success with learners. In relation to complex learning of the kind developed in writing educational essays you will need to work at interpreting the criteria, understanding what they mean and building them into your thinking. Criteria like ability to develop a justified personal stance, being analytical not merely descriptive, constructing effective educational arguments, and so on, need teasing out with examples and discussion. They are considered further below.

Another type of essay or assignment common in teacher education is the reflective evaluation of teaching plans. You might be asked to review plans for a set of mathematics lessons or any curriculum area. Here you would be expected to explain the ideas behind your plans, consider evidence about how they worked in practice, and then reflect on how your teaching might develop. Discussion of each aspect would need to demonstrate a grasp of relevant theory and research evidence, as well as practical judgement as a teacher. Other possible topics are curriculum development activities in a secondary school, fieldwork in geography, or applying some general idea like problem-solving or critical thinking to mathematics, science, or art and design.

Many reflective analyses require you to combine ideas about curriculum and curriculum principles (such as balance, coherence, progression) with ideas about effective teaching strategies, assessment methods, resourcing, and evidence of the effects of teaching on pupil learning. Faced with such tasks many students merely offer common-sense practical comments not analytical, theorised ones. You need both, however.

BEING ANALYTICAL AND DEVELOPING A PERSONAL STANCE

In the face of the deeply contested nature of educational ideas and practices, the interaction of practices and values, and the fact that much research does not have direct application to practical contexts, there is no point pretending there is some agreed science of education and teaching, some right answer. Students facing contexts with no right answer can be tempted to assume that any answer will do, that one opinion is as good as any other. This is not so, however. You need to live with uncertainty and work out the most convincing answer in the circumstances.

Some students are unsure about what alternatives exist to just reproducing others' ideas, using loosely paraphrased chunks, weakly linked together. Much better than such descriptive knowledge telling is where you include an overview, stronger links and more of your own knitting together of ideas from a range of sources, along with your own arguments. Best of all is where you really take charge of the essay, impose a structure to suit the material, provide a deep analysis, and a well-considered viewpoint or perspective. Try to get on the inside of the material, exploring the issues, evidence, arguments and theories in a deep and critical way, organising ideas and information to build your argument.

You are the one most knowledgeable about the context and need to develop practical professional judgement about this context, using the best available evidence of relevant factors. What is wanted is an authentic personal voice expressed by providing argument and evidence. You are seeking to argue a case based on reflective, critical analysis and bringing evidence, argument and logic to your writing and essay narrative. Prepare to look critically at the standard arguments and positions. It is this sort of essay writing that proves professionally and personally rewarding – even enjoyable!

Educational essays typically raise questions not only of fact but of meaning, and of aims, principles and values. Factual questions are a matter of evidence or research studies. In the absence of hard evidence, practical experience and judgement is necessary. Beware anecdotal evidence; look critically at experience asking how general and how typical of other classrooms it is. For research studies ask yourself how representative, how generalisable to other contexts they are. If it is a case study, consider what light it might shed on similar situations. Case studies don't normally aim at generalisation but illumination of similar cases. Practical judgement can be important here – a sense of the reality of classroom life, alert to the possible consequences of action and aware of how schools work. But remember that practice always implies some theory and different theories provide different criteria for deciding 'what works'. There is no pure practice.

Four different approaches to developing an essay script have been detected by Crème and Lea (1997). Some students just dive in anywhere to start writing, get a feel of the water and work it out from there. Others work separately at different sections as if making a patchwork quilt. Eventually they join the sections together neatly. Yet others develop a detailed plan, like meticulous architects with everything in its precise place. Finally, some gradually develop a grand plan in their heads, where it continues to brew for weeks before they eventually pour it all out onto paper. Which one are you? Perhaps you adopt different approaches to different essays. This shows admirably flexibility and it is unlikely that there is a fixed personal style.

TO QUOTE OR NOT TO QUOTE

Some students think they are expected to lard their educational essays with quotations from experts. This leads to some very poor essays. Students in social sciences typically see quotations as having four possible functions:

- adding authority;
- giving an academic tone or cachet to their writing;
- a way of 'bringing in theory' to otherwise descriptive writing or common-sense analysis of practice);
- a way of avoiding accusations of plagiarism, by acknowledging that the ideas are not their own.

None of these aims, however, strictly requires the use of quotation. Normal referencing and paraphrasing (putting the ideas briefly in your own words) will suffice and is usually better because more concise. Instead of saying 'According to Smith, "the best strategy for differentiation in this context is differentiation by expected outcome" and this is the approach I adopted' you can say: 'I used the strategy of differentiation by expected outcome. Smith (1963: 23) recommends this for these circumstances.' You need the reference to prevent the reader assuming the idea is yours. You do not need the actual quote; it doesn't add anything.

What then is the point of quoting in educational essays and assignments? There are three main uses. One is to put the ideas you want to discuss before the reader in the writer's own words. This, common in English literature essays, has potential in educational ones, though it is not exploited as much as it might be. Secondly, some writers have put certain points in very concise, elegant and telling ways and are worth quoting for the quality of writing and thinking. Lastly, it is sometimes important to quote the exact words of someone you interviewed (a pupil in a discussion, a parent or teacher) to give an authentic account of the ideas being expressed. Beware you do not pick the most obvious, even banal, points to quote. Basic ideas don't need authoritative quotation or reference. Sometimes students write things like: 'As Jones points out, "assessment tasks can have a very strong influence on teaching approaches." ' But this point is a self-evident one, obvious to any teacher at a moment's careful thinking. You don't need Professor Jones' authority, the quote or even the reference to convince the reader. Always ask yourself if a quotation provides new insights.

The fact that an acknowledged expert has said something does not make it valid or beyond criticism. Far from it. Official reports on education, regrettably, have long been a rich seam for anyone looking for statements based on spurious logic, empty rhetoric, confused meanings and dubious assertions. Official writings, like any other kind, need to be the focus of critical scrutiny, not unthinking acceptance.

Relying on extensive quotation can inhibit critical thinking. You might come across a section of writing that looks very promising and worth quoting at some length. It seems just to fit the bill and to add weight to your argument. If you find yourself so tempted, try putting the ideas concisely in your own words. You may well find (it happens often) that the ideas turn out to be less convincing than first appeared, and possibly even spurious.

Putting quotations in your own words is a very good discipline and aid to critical thinking. Quote only the words that are really telling – usually no more than a few lines – and don't let others' writing cut off your own thinking. Try to avoid a scissors-and-paste approach whereby loose paraphrases are strung together with selected quotations to structure an essay. This won't be your essay or your well-structured argument. It is in danger of becoming highly derivative or a work of plagiarism. Build your own argument; reference and quote only where it is apt. Above all, don't quote if you don't understand. Three lines of academic jargon are likely to look out of kilter with your normal writing and if you don't explain them you will fail to convince.

REFERENCING

There are three main reasons for referencing:

- to acknowledge the source of ideas that are not your own;

- to make public the source of evidence, for critical scrutiny;

- to aid interested readers to follow up further.

For the last two it is helpful to indicate a precise source. Suppose the ideas are on page 362 of a book by John Bull. It is helpful to write 'As Bull (2004: 362) argues . . .' If you just write 'As Bull (2004) argues . . .' then to find the section your reader may have to read through 362 pages of Bull!

This system of referencing is known as the Harvard system. It is simple and effective. In your script you give the author's name, date of publication and page number (if referring to a specific point as opposed to the general argument). In your bibliography you write the reference in full:

Kelly, A. V. (2004), The Curriculum (5th edition). London: Paul Chapman.

Note: surname(s) first, then initials, date, title, place of publication, publisher. To avoid later panic, keep careful details when taking a book out of the library and reading. For web pages include the full address of the page, not just the address of the site. This can be copied from the address bar (normally at the top of the browser). Add the date you accessed it because web pages are often modified later.

Other academic disciplines (for example history, English) have a tradition of using a system of footnotes and Latin referencing conventions. Historical, comparative and philosophical studies of education often suit this approach. In teacher education you are unlikely to need this but if you are used to it from a first degree in English or history you may find it easier to stick to what you know. Check with your course leader, however, in case they have a set requirement.

Students often ask how many different sources they are expected to use and how often should you reference in writing an essay? Two dangers need to be avoided: too little and too much. One way to get an idea of what is sensible is to see how the books you are reading do it. In a 2,500-word essay just four sources would be sparse, while more than twenty-five may make a reader wonder how thoroughly you had been able to read them. It is not a numbers game, however, but a matter of judgement in a context. Think of the principles of providing evidence, showing understanding of ideas and alternative views, and acknowledging sources, while maintaining a sensible approach which avoids referencing every second statement.

WRITING STYLE

In the light of what has been said above, your style should be formal but engaged, neither polemical nor coldly clinical, confident where appropriate but suspending judgement where evidence is lacking or issues are difficult to resolve. Beware of using extremist words like totally, absolutely, completely. They are rarely applicable in educational contexts where things are seldom black and white.

Some academic contexts traditionally discouraged the use of 'I' in essay writing, viewing it with suspicion as lacking objectivity and intruding personal opinion in place of established fact and rational, evidenced argument. A general trend towards encouraging the use of 'I' where appropriate is clear, however, and instructing students never to use 'I' seems difficult to justify for essays in the social sciences. Objectivity depends on quality of evidence and argument, not use of 'I'. Subjective ideas are not made objective by changing 'I noticed that' to a passive construction or impersonal voice such as 'It was observed that . . .' in reporting observations of children. Excessively passive writing is dull and should not be used to objectify opinions about which you are unconfident. Aim for a generally active voice but do use passive constructions when appropriate. Use 'I' sparingly, however, because otherwise the whole essay will be a series of 'I think . . . I think . . .'. Learn some other phrases which retain the personal voice like 'I shall try to demonstrate that . . .', 'Given the unreliability of this evidence the best strategy is surely. . .'.

A good essay will have a range of impressive features: careful thinking and research which thoroughly addresses the question, effectively documented and applied; a well-written piece of English, well organised and presented. Interweave sources rather than juxtaposing slabs from different authors. Check the relevance of content as you go along to ensure you are answering the question.

JARGON

In educational writing impenetrable jargon can be very off-putting. Jargon is specialised language or terminology associated with a particular subject or profession, often associated with obscurity and complexity of meaning and style. All professions and occupations tend to develop their own jargon but it is a particular problem in education.

One problem is that school jargon tends to differ from that of academics in universities and research centres. Teachers who remain unaware of their own school jargon express irritation at academic educational writing. Yet parents and the public can find school jargon obscure and one important task for schools is to communicate in ordinary terms with parents about curriculum, teaching and learning. The second problem is that studying education involves reading psychology, sociology, philosophy and educational research. Each has its own technical terms and style of discourse. There is a suspicion (not always unfounded in the social sciences) that obscure language is used to make simple ideas look difficult and complex for academic effect. Many academic texts are not written primarily for teachers in training but for other academics and are rarely exemplars of clear, powerful writing. Moreover, some official policy documents, while nowadays generally clear and accessible can be somewhat dulled by a necessary bureaucratic style.

When reading, the solution is to keep translating jargon into simpler terms using your own words. This becomes easier and less irritating with practice. You will find that your reading begins to make sense and is not really as difficult as it first seemed. When writing, use a clear, straightforward, active style in the best English you can muster. Don't be afraid to use technical terms but don't blind the reader with obscure jargon in an attempt to sound erudite.

BECOMING A BETTER WRITER

In exams and essays some students write much more concisely than others. Packing more ideas and information into the same space can make a big difference to an answer's overall quality. If you have learned to write concisely you are on to a winner, especially if you also have a good style. If not, it is worth working at these aspects. Some students find difficulty keeping to word limits. A simple strategy for cutting down your essay and improving the quality and conciseness of your writing is provided at the end of this chapter.

Written assignments provide an opportunity to improve your general writing ability and schools and teachers expect high standards of literacy from teaching students. Some claim they 'have good ideas but just can't put them down easily.' But in the arts form and content always interact. Certainly, for written assignments, learning to develop good ideas and to express them go hand in hand. An excellent range of books on writing good English is available and it is worth browsing before investing in one that suits you. You should find updated editions of Fowler's *Modern English Usage* and other guides in the university library. As a teacher you will need a good dictionary and you should use the thesaurus on your computer in writing assignments.

Both spoken and written English are constantly developing. Some usage considered bad English twenty years ago is perfectly acceptable today. Purists shudder at much modern writing, blaming poor education, sloppy thinking and a lack of care with grammar. Others argue that modern life requires quick, uncluttered communication and that this determines changes, many of which are irresistible and become 'good English.' Yet not anything goes. A poor grasp of spelling and the use of the apostrophe will give an impression of being ill-educated, as will not writing in proper sentences. Tutors and schools will question your ability to teach children the basics of grammar and punctuation.

What follows below is not a full survey but brief advice on how to make your work rapidly presentable and avoid the worst howlers. The points made here should help you understand the main problems, provide confidence and encourage you to read further to develop a stronger grasp of grammar and punctuation.

Spelling

Many students have no difficulty with spelling. A few, however, are unsure about some words commonly used in educational writing. Here is a list of words commonly misspelled by students in educational essays. If you are not confident about spelling you should attend to them because it will give a bad impression if, for example, you spell 'professional' with two fs, 'practice' as a verb with c not s, and so on.

Correct spelling	*Common mistake*
accommodation	only one m
definitely	definately (think finite)
occasionally	double s
separate	seperate
independent	-ant
argument	arguement (argue, but argument)
occurrence	-ance
practice/practise	teaching practice (noun) but practise (verb) the piano
professional	proffessional (should be only one f!)
fulfil	fulfill (only one l at the end)
committed	one t
embarrassing	one r
receive	ieve ('i before e except after c')

Learn to spell by reading widely, getting interested in and paying attention to words and thinking of yourself as a writer seeking to communicate with your audience. Think about grammar and proof read carefully.

A computer spell checker can lull you into a false sense of security. It won't pick up mistakes like 'there' for 'their', 'well-paste' teaching for 'well-paced' (an actual example) and common confusions like those listed below:

- lose (misplace) and loose (slack)
- affect (influence) and effect (result)
- principal (chief) and principle (rule or precept)

Words like criteria, phenomena and media are plural. The singular forms are criterion, phenomenon and medium. Data, strictly, is plural with datum the singular and hence you should say 'the data are' not 'the data is'. But many now say 'data is'. Language use is changing (just as we now say 'His stamina was – not were – remarkable'). At least remember to say 'the criterion . . .' if there is only one and 'the criteria . . .' if there are two or more.

More worrying for purists is the mixing of singular and plural in an effort to counter gender bias in writing. For example, it is still generally considered wrong to write: 'The teacher, in thinking about their role in leading discussion . . .' Some write 'their' because they don't want to write 'his' and 'his or her' sounds clumsy. This is now common in some popular books. But most still consider it formally wrong – and ugly – and you are strongly recommended to avoid this mistake. The simple, and best, solution is to write 'Teachers, in thinking about their role. . .'. This takes little effort and keeps your writing correct. Occasionally you will need to use 'his or her'. Other possibilities like s/he are inelegant and should be avoided. In spoken English, however, it has long been acceptable to say 'Ask the person to give their phone number' and written English may eventually follow suit, to the dismay of many.

Grammar and punctuation

Commas
Strike a balance between too few and too many commas. If you are not confident don't splatter commas around. If in doubt, leave the comma out, but determine to learn the effective modern use of commas. If your fault is using hardly any try to see where inserting a comma will help the reader draw breath and grasp your meaning easily. For example a comma after 'any' in the last sentence and after 'example' in this one would help.

Beware of joining what should be two separate sentences with a comma. Consider the following: 'I found the class difficult to control, they were very noisy.' You need a full stop after 'control' (and a capital at 'they'). They are two sentences, two complete thoughts each with a subject and verb. Joining them with a comma as one sentence is an elementary mistake which will make your writing look childish or ill-educated.

'Nevertheless' and 'however' are not conjunctions (but adverbs) and you can't just use a comma with them in mid-sentence. You need a full stop (or at least a semi-colon). Using a comma with however is a common mistake. When however is essentially in brackets you should of course write (for example) 'It is not, however, clear that. . .'. But you should not write 'He said he understood, however he made the same mistake again.' Here you need a full stop or semicolon before however. Nor can you write '. . . understood, however, he made the same . . .' (this is different from the bracketed use above).

Commas have four main uses:

- to separate items in a list: 'principles such as balance, coherence, breadth and progression.' Note that in lists there is usually no comma before the 'and' (but look up 'Oxford comma' in Fowler's English Usage);
- to separate out non-essential words or phrases: 'All the same, if a decision has to be made then . . .';
- to act as brackets: 'Mr Smith, the headteacher, explained that . . .' (note the two commas, one before, one after 'the headteacher');
- to separate multiple adjectives: 'pupils benefit from prompt, specific feedback'.

Semicolons and colons
If you are not confident you can get away without using these, and that may be the best strategy; but they do have a role in good writing which is not difficult to grasp.

A semicolon indicates a pause shorter than a full stop but longer than a comma. Use this to join two closely related sentences. Beware, however, of just using a comma here. It also helps in separating items in complex lists.

Exclamation marks
Avoid these in academic writing. Make your point forcefully in words.

Hyphens
Originally designed for compound words, hyphens can be useful for resolving ambiguities. Compare 'deemphasise' and 'de-emphasise', 'cooperate' and 'co-operate' (hyphen after the prefix). Practice is changing rapidly here with formerly hyphenated words like 'multi-media' becoming single words. Try to be consistent in using hyphens.

Quotation marks
Use for short quotations and reported speech but not to indicate slang. Don't write slang in essays. Find a better word or expression. If you quote more than twenty-five words you should normally indent the quote as a separate piece of text.

Apostrophes
The use of apostrophes is where many get very confused. In fact they are quite easy – if you keep a clear head. The basic rules are simple:

- if the possessor is singular add 's (teacher's book);

- if the plural ends in s add ' (pupils' books);

- if the plural does not end in s use 's (children's jotters).

Make the plural first, then the possessive (teacher, teachers, teachers'; child, children, children's).
    'Its' and 'it's' cause the most confusion and embarrassing mistakes. This is because another use of an apostrophe is to shorten words (it's for it is) and because with 'it' the possessive is 'its' not 'it's'. One way to prevent mistakes is never to shorten words in writing essays and therefore to use an apostrophe only for possessives (the boy's book, teacher's desk and so on). Hence in an essay you will never write 'it's' because you will never shorten 'it is' and for 'it' the possessive is 'its' ('its effect was surprising').

Sentences

Sentences should vary in length naturally, depending on what you want to say. Some will be short some medium, some long. The modern trend is for shorter sentences but variety is natural and important. Too many short sentences will make your writing childish and disjointed. Your sentences should vary to suit your material and developing argument.

Paragraphs

The aim is to break up the text for your reader. If paragraphs are too long, readers will find it difficult to grasp the meaning readily and to maintain attention. A natural balance and variety will emerge if you focus on explaining one idea clearly at a time and on helping the reader grasp the key points.

Normally each paragraph should focus on one main idea. Not all paragraphs will be of equal length, however, because some ideas need more explanation than others and judgement is required in breaking up a long stretch of writing. Often you need to recast your explanation and the flow of ideas.

End note: how to cut words in an essay

First version (eighty-seven words)
A learning style is a student's consistent way of responding to and using stimuli in the context of learning. There are various instruments used to determine a student's learning style. The first style to be discussed is VAK (Visual, Auditory, Kinaesthetic), which is derived from the accelerated learning world, and seems to be about the most popular model nowadays. Its main strength is that it is quite simple, which appeals to a lot of people. Its main weakness is that the research does not really support it.

Second version (forty-eight words)
(Produced by trying to cut every second word where possible without losing too much sense and changing some phrases quickly (like 'is' for 'seems to be about' and 'hence' for 'which makes it quite') and using dashes to keep the sense going at this stage.)

Learning style – student's consistent way responding to stimuli in learning. Various instruments to determine learning style. First, VAK (Visual, Auditory, Kinaesthetic), derived from accelerated learning – the most popular. Main strength – simple, which appeals to a lot; main weakness – research does not really support it.

Final version (after tidying up and recasting some phrases – thirty-nine words)
Learning styles (consistent approaches to learning tasks) can be variously categorised. The most popular classification, VAK (Visual, Auditory, Kinaesthetic), derives from accelerated learning theory. Its strength and appeal is simplicity and face validity, its main weakness unconvincing research evidence.

11 MAKING PRESENTATIONS

Shakespeare's contemporary, Ben Jonson, pointed out that 'talking and eloquence are not the same: to speak, and to speak well, are two things.' In other words, making an accomplished oral presentation is a real skill. It is an important and rewarding one in a teaching career. It is also eminently learnable: good advice, practice and feedback can quickly transform your presenting and set you on a path to continuing improvement.

A student remarked in a recent course evaluation: 'This programme works well if it gives me confidence as a teacher.' This struck home because universities tend to see their role as promoting understanding and helping students acquire analytic and critical thinking skills, looking closely at, perhaps too confident, assumptions about education and teaching. Yet uppermost in the student's mind – her test – was: 'Does it give me confidence as a teacher?' She knew that somehow, by June, she had to convince schools that she could confidently and competently teach a wide range of subjects, only one of which she had studied in her degree, to children from three to twelve. Of course, she wanted her training to provide not some vague, general assurance but proper professional confidence, based on understanding and skill. One of the best ways of developing this is to learn how to make a convincing oral presentation on teaching.

WHY PRESENTATIONS?

Oral presentations are playing an ever more important role in teacher education programmes because they

- develop professional communication;
- reinforce teaching skills;

- enable students to share ideas and experience in a short course;
- provide a strong test of understanding – and hence are a good assessment method;
- boost professional confidence;
- develop important transferable skills.

All teachers today need to develop effective professional communication. Most such communication is oral, not written. Written essays and assignments remain one good basis for assessing university studies, and developing educational writing and thinking skills. Practising teachers, however, don't actually spend much time on lengthy written communications. They do spend time talking with parents and with colleagues in school and staff development sessions. Anyone who can give an interesting and well judged talk to parents – about the teaching of reading or a forthcoming school trip, or explain clearly a pupil's performance in a particular subject – will soon be highly respected for these skills, and have an advantage in job interviews. Effective oral communication is a key professional competence and experience in oral presenting during teacher training is central to its development.

When you think about it, presenting is basically a form of teaching. Hence developing presentation skills is one way of reinforcing good teaching skills. It is further teaching practice – in a particular, focused context. Presenting well requires taking account of your audience's knowledge and interests, structuring your talk to suit your audience and using resources effectively. These are precisely the skills of planning a good lesson. Indeed, teachers can learn much about effective teaching by observing how skilled media presenters structure and deliver news bulletins, weather forecasts, and documentaries. Presentations are an excellent way of enabling students to share experiences. The words of wisdom in your essay will be read only by the marker. However, five students each presenting in turn to the other four on a reading programme they used on placement enables them to tap quickly into wider experience, and presenting also prepares well for sharing ideas and experiences once you qualify.

Research shows presentations are a powerful assessment mode, a strong and authentic test of understanding educational theory and practice. Presenting encourages deep thinking, a clear, powerful focus on the core argument, the most telling and convincing evidence, and clear structuring.

You have to know what you are talking about. In an essay it is possible (students have been known to succumb!) to write things you don't understand, hoping the marker will assume you do from the complex jargon in which you couch your ideas. You can't get away with a surface grasp of ideas in a presentation where you will face an unknown audience and don't know what questions you may be asked.

Finally, oral presenting is a transferable skill, useful in all sorts of contexts in and out of teaching; and teacher education is now expected to develop such transferable skills. All these factors make presentations a cornerstone for building your confidence in professional communication.

HOW TO GIVE A REALLY GOOD TALK

Nowadays students come into teacher training with a considerable variety of experience in presenting. Some have never given a formal talk in their life; a few mature students come from jobs which involved training other employees to present. Most postgraduates have some experience, mainly in university seminars, and in less formal situations, such as sports clubs, religious organisations and social groups. Surveys indicate, however, that few students have read books on presenting, or had systematic training. In university seminars some idea about what is expected and how to achieve it emerges through peer observation as seminar papers are delivered week by week.

Presentations today come in all shapes and sizes: business presentations to large audiences or just two colleagues; educational talks to parents; seminars and lectures in universities;

news bulletins, weather forecasts and political broadcasts; after dinner talks and wedding speeches. They range from off-the-cuff remarks to professionally produced multi-media presentations. Whatever kind of talk, certain fundamental principles apply. If you want to give a good talk you have first to grasp these principles and then apply them to the particular context. There are seven such fundamentals underlying all good public speaking:

1. Be your (best) self

2. Be precise about your purpose

3. Address your audience's interests and concerns

4. Master your subject

5. Structure for listeners

6. Use resources imaginatively

7. Learn to deliver confidently

NATURAL AND PROFESSIONAL

A balance has to be struck between being natural and being professional. You need to avoid putting on a special, telephone or plummy voice – the last thing you want is to appear remote, stiff or very formal. It is equally ineffective to talk in an informal, chatty approach (one tendency when nervous) as if discussing over a lazy coffee. You have to find a way to make contact with your audience but remember you are trying to lift your audience in some way through your presentation, offering them new ideas and insights, not just sharing their current problems and perceptions. Be yourself but raise your normal conversational and interactional game to meet the occasion.

Think of your presentation as set in a slightly formal, professional context, not an informal student context, which you might find comforting but which will not help you develop confidence in speaking to, say, a group of parents. Try to give your presentations a professional edge while remaining natural. As one television reporter put it, presenting 'is an acting job – act natural!' So speak in your own voice, wear your 'own clothes' and don't pretend to be someone else.

When student teachers begin presenting many of them ignore dress, as if personal presentation is not important. Some even slouch casually on a table, eyes down on their A4 script, reading their talk. After several presentations, however, they usually come well groomed, have thought about clothes and stand naturally erect. They exude a real confidence in themselves because of their personal presentation and the thoroughness with which they have prepared their talk. They talk naturally but it is their best selves they are putting forward and the audience responds with interest and respect.

HANDLING NERVES

Nerves are common and natural and can be made to work for you. Almost all good speakers have some nerves before taking the podium. Some famous actors experience major bouts of nerves before performances but it does not prevent them from making stunning careers out of acting. Controlled tension is well known to enhance athletic performance. As one business presenter remarked, 'It's good to let a bit of adrenalin kick in; it gives an edge to your performance.'

Public speaking nerves stem from five main fears:

- drying up;

- boring the audience;

- facing disasters – technology troubles, dropping notes, mis-judging the audience;

- appearing a fool – through lack of knowledge and making intellectual blunders;

- wanting to excel but doubting you are up to it.

There are, fortunately, simple answers to all these fears. They can be overcome, usually quite quickly.

Take drying up: it is very possible to learn how to time a talk properly, have enough material, and have note cards to which you can easily refer in case you lose the thread. Most speakers actually speak too long, not too short.

Boring the audience is certainly a danger. To avoid it, you need to connect with the audience's interests and concerns and use resources to liven up your talk. Without these features your speech may well be dry and disappointing. All this can be learned. Another factor was well put by Voltaire: 'The secret of being a bore', he said, 'is to tell everything.' The trouble is that having thoroughly researched your subject you feel you must put all you know across, every blessed detail. But this will not enthuse your audience. They want ideas presented concisely and in a lively manner, with space to think their own thoughts about the subject. Try to see a talk more as a sketch, not an exhaustive, and exhausting, report on your thinking. Yet your sketch needs to have real interest and significant detail or it will not engage attention. Once more it is a matter of balance.

Disaster can strike anyone but you need to realise that audiences want you to succeed. They do not want you to fail or look a fool and will feel for you if things go wrong. They come hoping to be enlightened and perhaps be pleasantly entertained in the process, not to sit through a presentation that fails. That will embarrass them as well as you. The audience is your friend, not foe. Humour is often a quick solution to disasters, which are rarely as bad as they seem. Suppose your notes fall on the floor. Why not say 'Oh dear; I've hardly begun my talk and already it has fallen completely flat!' You'll get a laugh, sympathy and respect for being able to handle the situation with such aplomb. Carefully pick up your notes and continue from where you left off. Use a similar approach to other potential disasters. Above all be prepared to handle any crisis coolly and calmly. Don't get flustered.

Presentation assignments in teacher education are not trying to catch you out, though they are strong tests of your knowledge. This is precisely why they are good experiences and help develop understanding. In preparing for a talk aim to leave enough time to develop a good understanding and avoid a last minute rush which can leave you exposed. You also need to learn to handle questions confidently. Remember, you can't be expected to know everything. Don't launch into another presentation but answer clearly and concisely and only expand if the questioner obviously wants this. Adopt a positive approach to audience questions as an opportunity to engage with other interested people in exploring the issues you have been talking about.

Remember that most people look only 10 per cent as nervous as they feel inside. Experienced TV presenters point out that while on the surface they may appear calm and elegant as swans, below the 'waterline' they are paddling furiously. This works day in, day out for professionals; it can for you.

There are proven techniques for controlling nerves which everyone can learn, including deep breathing exercises and imagining success. Try lying in a bath and imagining the audience enjoying your talk, smiling or applauding at the end and the satisfaction you feel as you gather up your notes. These techniques give confidence if the proper preparation is in place. Two other measures can also help. One is to memorise the opening and close. At least you will begin and end well – and this is what audiences remember most. The other is to focus on your message, not your performance. This has been shown to make a significant difference to nervousness during delivery. Forget yourself, and concentrate on getting your important ideas across to your audience.

Take all opportunities to gain experience. What builds confidence is seeing that the world does not come to an end if you make a mistake, forget your lines, if the computer or DVD does not work. You learn how a presentation works, how it is put together, what makes it flow. You realise that audiences, mostly, don't bite. People still smile at you and speak to you the next day. However much your mind is on your supposed disaster, their minds are on their own concerns.

STAND AND DELIVER

Few people pay the attention they should to stance. Yet it is the foundation of clear and confident speaking and you need to understand why. Posture and voice are connected. Both are important in teaching and in presenting and in learning to present you can adopt a professional approach to them.

The crux in relation to stance is to place both feet firmly on the floor, in contact with Mother Earth as it were. This will enable you to keep yourself erect with a natural posture and your shoulders straight. All this helps voice production and eye contact, prevents tension, induced by nervousness, in your neck and shoulders, which leads to voice problems. You'll be amazed if you look closely at students (and indeed teachers and lecturers) presenting at how convoluted leg movements can become. Some hop from one foot to another, or twist their legs in a plait; others lean back on one foot or on the podium for support. Some just can't stay still and walk to and fro as they speak. All this is done unconsciously because of nerves and poor habits. It does not help you present well.

Pace of speaking is important too. Nerves naturally make you speak fast but speakers usually slow down as they get into their stride and tension decreases. Too slow and deliberate a speed may make you comfortable but will bore your audience. A slightly fast, but still measured, approach can work well. Learn to take a cue from the audience about what speed enables them to take it all in and maintains interest. The goal is to develop a good momentum, not a dull, pedestrian gait. Varying pace, judging what your material requires, is a skill you can develop with experience. Try to avoid a monotone voice. It will vary naturally if you focus not just on getting through your talk but on trying to get your message across in a convincing way. Aim to become aware of your voice and its reception, clarity and diction. All these aspects can be worked on once you have a good posture.

Eye contact is a crucial test of a good speaker. Nerves make speakers avoid eye contact and when they try to overcome this they resort to an awkward pattern of eye movements. What kind of notes you use is crucial. A4 sheets flap around and your eyes go down. Smaller note cards can be held and viewed in a way that maintains good eye contact with the audience. Cover the whole audience, not just one person for the entire speech. Talk for a few minutes to one then to another but don't constantly flit from one person to another.

A lectern or podium can be a useful aid at first (hold the sides firmly) but don't hide behind it. Face up to your audience. Don't bury your head in your notes or stare out of the window when speaking. The audience will not turn out to be ogres. Find a friendly face – there will at least be one! Experience is a great teacher here; so get as much as you can.

The main thing is to convey enthusiasm for your topic and engagement with it. Make your talk sound said, not read. You are not reading a lecture or an essay to the audience. Note cards are a great help here if you write just headings and phrases, not a full script. This will enable you to maintain eye contact and talk without losing your thread or ideas and give a more natural feel to you speech. If using PowerPoint, use note cards too, and look at the audience, not the projector or the screen.

STRUCTURE

In preparing your talk, you need to understand your material well and also to structure it in a way that your listeners will find makes sense and is easy to follow. Think like a listener and remember your audience is hearing it for the first time. Prepare the opening, the main body and the close. The opening and close are separate, top-and-tail, pieces. These do quite different jobs from the main structure and need to be carefully planned. Audiences tend to remember them (known in psychology as the primacy and recency effects).

Opening

The opening has to grab the audience's attention and convince them the talk will be worth listening to. Remember they don't have to listen, they could just sit there thinking about something else, day-dream or whatever. Audiences have short attention spans. There are various kinds of attention grabber (or hook) – an arresting quote, a startling fact, posing a problem or challenge.

The opening should give an overview of how your talk is structured and what it will contain. Try to convey the essence of the points you will be making. Don't just list the topics you will deal with.

A third aspect of the opening is to communicate the central thought of your talk. You need to have a central thought which gives your talk overall coherence. You should convey this orally not put it on an overhead, because it is very important that the audience focuses on you at this point.

For a good talk you need to have something you consider important to communicate to your audience. But it has to link clearly to their concerns and perspectives. It is in the overlap, where your message and their concerns meet, that you will find the source of a good talk. You need, therefore, to find out about your audience's interests and concerns. Think about how your talk can benefit your audience. Will it explain a teaching approach they might use with profit, or give them insights into pupils' learning difficulties, provide ideas for more imaginative teaching or what?

Traditionally, speeches have one of four purposes: to inform, persuade, inspire, or entertain. Academic presentations are usually some mix of the first two or three. If you can present your ideas in a lively way this is a bonus for listeners.

Close

The close has a quite different function. It is to sum up briefly then leave your audience with a memorable thought or challenge which drives home your central message and motivates them to follow up your ideas – perhaps by reading or discussing further, or trying something out in the classroom. Two things to avoid are, first, saying 'And finally' then taking the audience's suddenly increased attention as a cue for launching into another speech; and, secondly, apologizing. This is not the time or place. Finish strongly, decisively and quickly.

Body

The body of the speech needs to be carefully structured, to break up your material so that listeners can easily take it in. Though it may sound arbitrary and dogmatic, you are strongly advised to have three main sections for your talk. Perhaps you think your material suits four or six. Research suggests, however, audiences prefer odd numbers, perhaps because they give a more rounded feel.

Seven main points will be too many and even five is near the limit. If you have seven, after the first two your audience will think 'we've only covered two; still five to cover. How long will this go on?' Always try to be shorter than the audience dared hope. You will have greater impact, better attention and their grateful thanks. You can probably convey your ideas more insightfully and forcefully in a short speech than a long one. Normally then, aim to collapse your ideas into just three sections. A speaker can probably only say one main thing well (broken into about three parts) in any talk.

In structuring a talk, speakers often just think in terms of an agenda they will cover. Many presentation remits in higher education encourage this because the remit lists aspects students are expected to cover. Structuring naturally follows this and you end up with six or seven sections or agenda items. However there are many possibilities for structuring a talk. Following an agenda is only one and probably the least interesting one for an audience. Here are some possibilities (see Weissmann 2004):

- problems/solutions;
- compare and contrast;
- issues/actions;
- case study (story line).

Thus you could identify three key problems you face in geography fieldwork, managing a difficult class or whatever, and explain the solution you arrived at for each. Issues/actions is similar though the actions may not have resolved the issues. In reporting developments, comparing then with now for a number of features often works well. If it is a case study, telling it as a story with a clear beginning, middle and end is likely to capture the audience's attention.

In developing the detail you need to be clear about the main points of each section and have good examples, analogies, vivid images and visuals; and smooth links between sections. If you just offer abstractions your audience will find it hard to keep attending.

CREATING VISUAL IMPACT

The main point is to keep the focus on yourself as presenter so that the audience attends to the ideas you are conveying. Visuals should enhance and support your talking, not take over. Don't confuse a presentation with a document. Don't expect your audience to do three things at once – listen to you speak, study your visual and read your handout. Generally, leave handouts until the end.

Visuals

Visuals undoubtedly have positive, but also potentially negative, effects. Well-judged visuals used sparingly at key points when they can clarify difficult points or make them convincing and memorable will enhance a presentation. Some listeners will appreciate a model, diagram or chart to clarify a process but remember not all will. It is one way of taking account of your listeners' learning style preferences. Not all are predominantly auditory learners. Have one or two telling visuals aids. Use pictures or diagrams if they are good ones. Sometimes an informal drawing will work well and you don't need to be a Picasso to make an effective visual. Found pictures can often make a real impact and it can be interesting to search for them. Many resort happily to Clip Art, but this is rarely impressive and has become rather hackneyed.

Text slides

These are useful for providing an overview (showing the wood as well as the trees), the core ideas and basic bullets, a summary and quotations.

In presenting, the slogan 'less is more' certainly applies, especially to visual aids and PowerPoint charts. The important thing is to de-clutter your slides. Here we come to the worst fault in modern computer presentations. Audiences have been deluged with slide after slide of detailed information and bullet points. It is easy, however, to cut these down and increase understanding, impact, interaction and listening.

A picture may be worth a thousand words but don't put up a slide which is in effect a picture of a thousand words. Cut out extraneous material. 'Can you put it on a T-shirt?' is a good motto in considering slide content.

An audience can't listen to you and read a text slide at the same time unless it is very brief. So if you put up a long slide filled with full sentences and then talk through this to the audience it is going to be caught between listening and reading. Some will read much faster than others and if you remove the slide before some have finished reading or taking notes you will upset them.

There is a much better way. Adopt the 'less is more' philosophy and discipline yourself to ensure no more than five lines per slide, no more than five words per line and use phrases not full sentences. Weissmann (2004) points out that doing this cuts down on the number of eye sweeps the audience requires to take in your visuals and so enables them to keep focusing on what you are saying while taking your slides in at a glance. If you have brief phrases or even single words it will help the audience keep your theme in mind and listen to you. Then if you talk naturally to them they will be helped by both the visual verbal and your natural talk. They will remark that you are easy to listen to if you talk at a level they can understand, with examples and analogies.

Make your slides clear and simple. Remember you'll need a font size of 24–26 to be seen clearly and that a 'sans serif' font will be easier to read on screen. Cut all irrelevant material. Use a consistent grammatical style in constructing phrases. Slides full of abstract words are unhelpful. You need examples or concrete images to make things come alive. Memorable presentations so often involve an image or analogy which stays in the mind.

CONCLUSION

Presentations are developing rapidly and the future is clearly a multimedia one, both in and out of the classroom. With developments in ICT, the skills and techniques of teaching and presenting are now increasingly similar. Aim to get as much experience of the potential and current problems of such multimedia presenting as possible.

The basic skills and principles of presenting remain, however, as does the need to take charge of your own development as a presenter. Presenting is eminently learnable and can be richly rewarding. It is not an end in itself but a key aspect of your modern teaching role as a communicator, whether to pupils, parents or colleagues.

12 MANAGING YOUR TIME

In every occupation there are several aspects that you have to learn to organise and juggle with. Otherwise pressure mounts and robs you of the space and time to enjoy your role, play it well and find it fulfilling. You need to be aware how these issues arise in teaching and develop strategies to handle them.

As a class teacher you will face many unexpected changes to plans. It is in the nature of the job. For example, in a primary school the fire service, or a parent skilled in using a digital camera, may come to visit at short notice, having had to cancel previous arrangements. The time newly set aside then overruns because the children become really interested. The lessons of that day somehow have to be squeezed into the next day. The curriculum has to be covered because there is pressure from above to do so; the lessons can't just be missed out. This is the reality teachers have to cope with. You need to be very flexible and able to think quickly about time use.

In addition, there are many imprecisely scheduled events for which you need to prepare and make room. Although on the horizon at the start of a term, their detailed timing is likely to be forthcoming only at short notice. There might be a book week, harvest festival, puppet theatre visit, and parents' literacy evening, school photos. Such events will regularly occur and you need to find a way of responding which keeps you in control, maintains your spaces and stops you rushing from crisis to crisis.

Furthermore, as is publicly acknowledged, teachers can face considerable workload pressure and can feel stressed by constant new initiatives, inspections, paperwork and performance targets. Learning how to resist needless and unacceptable workload pressure is vital for effective and confident teaching. The key to this is a clear grasp of the principles and values of modern time-management thinking, because these principles are essentially about managing workload to achieve personal and professional goals and priorities, and a good work/life balance. There is still a background culture of teachers staying late in school, working all hours and of teaching tending to take over your life. It seems to have originated, paradoxically, in a more relaxed era. Teaching is certainly an absorbing job, not a 'nine-to-five' one; but today the 'working all hours' approach needs to be challenged and replaced by a more effective and healthy approach to teaching, leisure and life away from school.

Consider all the things you have to do as a student teacher. Only part of your week will be timetabled. Apart from attending classes, you have to make sense of lecture notes, write essays, give presentations, read widely, prepare lessons for placement, search the web for teaching ideas, write up your placement teaching file, use the student e-mail conference and network with other students. You might have a part time job, possibly children, domestic commitments. You need some social life. You may also have a hobby, sporting or artistic pursuit.

Realistic and positive time planning and management are the way forward here. Time management is not an inborn skill any more than is organising your room or managing your finances. Few are naturally good at it and most have learned some poor habits. These need to be unlearned and better approaches developed for your own good, relationships with family and friends, and the benefit of pupils and colleagues in school. Most who are effective have worked at it and eventually learned the hard way through crises and frustrations; or have been lucky enough to have models and mentors who have helped them learn the habits and rewards from young. It is never too late to learn, however.

It is important to get one thing clear from the start in approaching time management. It is not a set of techniques to help you do everything faster – and therefore able to cram in even more work each day. Rather it means learning a sane and balanced approach to the demands made on your time; focusing on becoming aware of your aims as a student, a teacher, and in your personal life; and learning how to plan your use of time to achieve these goals. Time management needs to be learned because modern life, culture and technology put unhealthy pressures on study time as a student in higher education and in your professional life, whatever job you are in.

If you think you are already a good time manager, ask yourself the following questions and answer them carefully. Do you ever wonder where the day went, find yourself rushing to meet deadlines, find that tasks take longer than you fondly imagined they would, regularly mislay things, find yourself fighting crisis after crisis? Does your workload regularly build up on you? How much time did you spend with family and friends last week? Would they agree with your estimate? Is there something you didn't do yesterday you would like to have done? Was it important, did you forget, run out of time, put it off? Did you make a clear plan to do it? Why not? Do you set aside time for emergencies or just hope they won't occur?

Once you have some experience of placement in school, ask yourself the following. In the classroom on placement do you do things pupils could have done themselves? When asked for help by a pupil do you automatically stop what you are doing to help? Do you use your classroom time to your satisfaction and feel in control? What one thing might you do which, if you did it regularly, would make a big difference to your work as a teacher? For example, think about making time to talk individually to each pupil at some point in the day.

WHY INVEST IN TIME MANAGEMENT?

Time management is something to invest in. It requires effort to get a good return and so you need to consider why it is worth investing and exactly what returns you can expect. There are three very good reasons why you should invest. It will put you in control of your time, thus developing professional confidence and satisfaction; it will help you teach better by focusing on what is important in teaching; and it will prove a good defence against workload pressure.

Time management quickly pays rich dividends through some simple, but disciplined, moves. As with learning generally, you can improve by reflective practice, looking critically at results and careful planning to do better next time.

PLANNING YOUR TIME

Consider all the things in your life you need time for – family and friends, your job (or studies while a student), interests, commitments and personal space. All these need to be taken into account in realistic time planning. This does not mean stopping being creative or spontaneous but rather making space in your life for these in a planned way. To fail to do this usually means they remain vague ideals that succumb quickly to the pressures of time; and so your hopes and good intentions are never fulfilled.

Within the constraints of the fixed commitments you face, a first step is to decide your priorities and then set realistic goals you want to achieve, taking into account what you can reasonably manage in the time available. This will normally mean you need to trim your ambitions for the short term. But it will enable you to make a more reality-based plan for achieving your goals in the longer term, and enable you to focus clearly on some important goals immediately.

When considering your teaching role or work as a student it is useful to make a distinction between tasks where you can be pro-active and those where you have to be reactive. Try as much as possible to be pro-active, deciding what you want and need to do, and how, not just waiting for work to be landed on you. Plan adequate time for these pro-active tasks and cut down your goals if the time seems impracticable. Secondly, leave sufficient space for tasks where you will have to be reactive. For regular routine work – marking, writing reports, schemes of work and lesson plans – you need to think out ways of doing these efficiently and well. All this means deciding what has to be done, when it can be done, what can't be done in the time and adjusting plans once you've taken stock of what is possible. As a teacher you will need to plan goals for your pupils' learning as well as for yourself as a working professional. Try to deadline all jobs.

Good time management itself takes time and so you need to plan time for time management. This will not be wasted. In practice it will free-up time. Set aside time to plan, to organise, to train pupils for delegation, to monitor and review your use of time. Once you have a system going, even fifteen minutes a day will prove a good investment, freeing up time that would otherwise be unproductive and which you can now use, not to cram in more activities but to work steadily on your priorities, or just give yourself personal space.

THE THREE 'P'S

We are now ready to consider three common obstacles to being a good time manager. You need to face up to these and work through them. You can think of them as the three Ps.

Parkinson's Law

The first of the three Ps is Parkinson's Law. Few students in higher education know this law, which is a pity because appreciating it and taking steps to avoid its effects are fundamental to controlling time. Parkinson's Law refers to a humorous, but very insightful, observation about the way in which people tend to approach big tasks like writing an essay, completing a project, and also regular activities like conducting a meeting. As Parkinson (1958) put it: 'Work expands to fill the time available for its completion'. If you have an essay due in three weeks it may well take you three weeks. If it is due in one week it will take one week at most. It will have to!

But why should you be tied to such time-scales? The person setting the essay or assigning the work probably did not judge it would take that time, or that the meeting required three hours, or that the project would take eight weeks to complete.

There are other reasons for these time lines – sheer tradition, advance communication of deadlines to aid planning, and so on. With any such tasks, you should ask not how long you have to do this but how long it will take to be done as well as it needs to be done. Then set aside that time and try to stick to it. Most are poor at judging how long a task will take and at sticking to plans. It is easier to say 'It's due next month so I've a whole month to think about it' and then spend three weeks half-heartedly doing it until near the deadline you panic and abandon other commitments to focus on this big, and now urgent, task.

Of course it is important to know essay and other deadlines well in advance so that you can let ideas float around the back of your mind, germinate properly and gradually mature. But you also need to try to judge well how long writing it up will take, and how important a priority it is. You need to plan a set time for it, aiming to complete it before the deadline and with spare time built in for emergencies.

Keen students sometimes assume that in order to do the best possible job they need to use all the time available. This is a mistake for two reasons. You need some space for other things and will not work to your peak if you are forever at full concentration on your project or essay. You may also find life has passed you by. Moreover, you need to avoid the trap of perfectionism, the second P. There will be particular short periods of time when we need to focus firmly, shutting all other aspects out; but not all the time, even in a one-year post-graduate course.

Plan to finish your essay or pupil reports at least two days early and to use the freed time for something else you want to do – leisure or another interesting task. This is an example of taking control of your time, making your own decisions about time needs and use. One reason people are typically poor at estimating the time required for tasks is insecurity about demanding tasks. Reflective disciplined practice and determination to be realistic leads to improvement – and eventually space to do the other things you want.

Some insist that they work best up against a deadline or

crisis. Undoubtedly in these contexts some people find they focus sharply and generate their best ideas. But if this is you it will pay to imagine a crisis well before the deadline and discipline yourself to focus. Equally often such crisis working produces unsatisfactory work, much worse than you might fondly imagine, and causes problems for colleagues.

To sum up, don't let the task expand to fill the available time. Deadline it and discipline yourself to stick to it. If it goes over then next time remember how much it overran. Optimism about what we can achieve leads us to underestimate the time it will take. But this is one area where it is important to be a realist not an optimist, because optimism in this context tends to mask insecurities about how much effort a task really needs. The best way forward in such circumstances is hard realism not self-deception. This also applies to the next P, perfectionism.

Perfectionism

Aiming to be perfect looks like a virtue but so often becomes a vice. Many people approach their work with an ideal of the perfect job, the perfectly completed assignment. Perhaps this results from being drilled into always seeking high achievement. High achievement is laudable – don't get me wrong – but perfectionism is not the way to it. Excessive perfectionism is misguided. You will not reach your goals or realise your aims through it.

There are two problems with excessive perfectionism. First it relies on the myth of the perfect task. Yet there is no such thing as the perfect worksheet, essay, lesson plan, exam answer. There is always room for improvement. You will never have got it totally right. The very concept is misguided because there are several good ways of doing things and all answers have strengths and weaknesses. Secondly you are constrained by time and resources. There is not enough time to do everything to perfection. Indeed, focusing on perfect task completion takes valuable time away from other, more important, tasks. It is easier to aim for perfection in simple tasks but these may not be the most important ones; and they waste time (which should be devoted to your key roles) on a fruitless quest for perfection, kidding yourself you have high standards and are a dedicated, disciplined worker. It is a misuse of your time and energy.

Perfectionism is generally unachievable, frustrating and can make you obsessive. However, there is a more worthwhile and achievable goal. Aim not to be perfect but to be excellent. This is a different mind set altogether. Excellence is achievable, gratifying and healthy, so long as you are realistic – excellent given the circumstances of time and resources. But be careful not to shy away from aiming to be excellent because of another, not unknown, failing – the fear of success.

Procrastination

The third P is procrastination, putting off things you know you should be doing. It is rightly labelled 'the thief of time.' Most people procrastinate – in universities advice sessions usually draw a crowd – but often over different things, probably because the roots of procrastination lie in individual dislikes and insecurities. If this is a significant problem for you, rest assured that you are not alone by a long chalk.

What kinds of tasks do people tend to put off? One kind is those on a large scale – major projects, complex tasks. While you may have an initial motivation for a big project, soon the magnitude of the task leads to delayed planning and action and you spend the time day-dreaming instead of buckling down. You entertain the conceit of a grand idea of what you will achieve but nothing much materialises. Secondly, people avoid getting on with tasks they find difficult, fear they'll fail in, or find unpalatable. Many are personally uncomfortable with tasks like sorting out a quarrel, complaining, resolving interpersonal issues with colleagues, friends or family. Thirdly, people tend to put off tasks they see as chores and don't enjoy. These may often be fairly routine and not partic-

ularly important but still necessary – or perhaps are important but have aspects they don't get much of a buzz from.

All these tasks thieve time because they prey on the mind
and don't leave you free to get on with other things. You find
excuses like making another coffee, having a digestive biscuit,
leafing through notes; or find yourself doing trivial, time-
wasting things, not active productive ones. You need to find a
way to face up to these and get them out of the way.

For big tasks it may help to use the salami technique, slicing
up the task into a number of smaller tasks. Like salami, they
are easier to digest one slice at a time. Often such large tasks
prove simpler than you thought. But beware of too fragmented an approach. You need to see the whole picture, for
example an essay as a whole, not just an amalgam of shorter
sections.

What about difficult and distasteful tasks? 'Do it now' is a
good philosophy in many cases. Difficult tasks don't get easier
if you delay and peace of mind comes from quickly getting
them out of the way. Besides, fears are often unfounded. In a
few cases the best thing is in fact to do nothing; some issues
evaporate. Batch chores if possible. You can even begin to
enjoy some chores and get satisfaction by learning how to do
difficult things with dispatch.

MASTER THE URGENT/IMPORTANT MATRIX

In any work or study situation tasks can be grouped into one
of four categories:

- urgent and important;
- urgent but not important;
- not urgent but important;
- not urgent nor important.

Of course there are degrees of importance and urgency. The
secret to good time management lies in the 'not urgent but

important' category. Some things have no real deadline but may be very important. In fact they are often the core of the role. Think about this in relation to classroom teaching.

Here is a summary of how to manage these different kinds of tasks:

Urgent and important – do as soon as possible.

Urgent but not so important – try to batch and to hold till a space occurs.

Not urgent and not important – bin these and do more useful and important things.

Not urgent but important – plan quality time for these as a priority; keep this time sacrosanct.

One problem is that some things become urgent and important because of crises which arise through poor organisation or external factors. Hence these things have to be done as a priority; but you need to prevent a crisis occurring next time. In learning time management, you will need to learn also to handle the results of poor time management until you can improve. After a crisis plan clearly how to avoid this recurring. It may mean cutting back on pet projects and planning space for emergencies.

Some things are urgent but not important. For example many e-mails are in this category (e-mail conferences for teaching students are now common). You should respond quickly – it helps the person who sent the e-mail, is polite and will earn you thanks and respect for being well organised. But many e-mails are probably not important. It is well worth batching these and similar tasks, like photocopying, library visits, replenishing stationery and food supplies, and getting a head of steam up. Keeping a regular slot for such work keeps you in control.

Not urgent, not important tasks look easy to handle but are not. For one thing, most feel guilt at being asked to bin them. You think: 'These have arrived on my desk. I have to tackle them, to respond.' But why? Try to bin quickly. Much paper work and certainly junk mail falls into this category. Secondly, however, you are often happy to do these because they are not taxing and you pretend to yourself you are working. Yet they prevent action on more important and useful tasks. You should feel good when you ditch these and make space for more important activities.

How you handle the last category, not urgent but important, is what distinguishes good from bad time managers. It tends to be the first casualty when a crisis arrives because they are not urgent no one will notice if you don't do them. You can delay without getting into immediate trouble. But the fact is that you then tend to neglect the core of your role or work and what makes it all worthwhile and interesting. Set aside key time and stick to it; don't get sucked into other demands which arise and you feel obliged to do just because you've been asked or because they come along. This is the place to hold the line. Stand firm and keep your time sacrosanct or secure the time very soon elsewhere by ditching something else.

OTHER TIME WASTERS

There are several other time wasters, all of which need to be dealt with firmly in a disciplined way. Frequent interruptions can make for very poor time use, in the classroom and outside. Try to do one thing at a time and finish it or at least a clear section of it if you can. Constantly having to pick up the thread of something is very inefficient. Think about how to handle requests for help from pupils, train them in independence and remain proactive in class.

How organised you are seems a matter of personal style. Some need tight control to be comfortable. Others are quite the opposite; unless there is a relatively loose structure they feel constrained and uncomfortable. A good strategy is to be basically organised without going to extremes and remain open without being chaotic. Biting the bullet of clearing your desk or working space and getting organised can aid both types. Personal disorganisation usually leads to constantly mislaying things, a great time-waster. Don't make a meal of getting organised, however. Once you've felt the benefits of a clear working space for a few weeks you are unlikely to put up with major disorganisation again.

Doing other people's jobs can happen in class, with your own children, with working colleagues and friends. Training pupils in independence saves time in the long run but needs an initial investment and discipline. Encouraging independence and personal growth can reduce any feelings of guilt – for example if, as a mature student, you are not doing as much for your children as before you began your course. Often people remark 'It's easier to do it myself.' This is probably true in a crisis or the short term; but afterwards make plans to prevent this becoming a habit.

A skill most find hard to face up to is saying no. There is an important difference of course between saying no positively, politely but firmly and just refusing tasks and opportunities with an eye to an easy life. No one wants a colleague or subordinate who does not give and take, is not committed to the job or is unwilling to do his or her share. But neither will you be a good team member if you prove an easy touch for any task and consequently overload yourself, so that you don't do anything well and create bottlenecks for others. Learn to say no positively and to have a good time-plan so that you can explain why you should not take on the proposed task. Learning to say no to yourself is often the core problem – being realistic about what you can take on without detriment to your effectiveness.

Once a term at least, review you use of time with a view to making real improvements. Reflect on what you planned, what actually happened and why. Consider how you could sort things for next time. Possible factors in ineffective use of time are poor prediction of time needs, poor control of interruptions, inability to say no, disorganisation, procrastination, and so on, as identified above. Some may find it helpful to observe their use of time in a time log, but for others this is a chore and a distraction from clear thinking about what needs to be sorted. The main questions cover how well your time was used, and how realistic your planning was. If you are having real difficulties, focus on time-managing one task really well.

HANDLING A CRISIS

If you are faced with a crisis you need to handle it effectively first and then reconsider your time management to ensure it does not recur. However, handling a crisis requires special measures. The first is this: don't treat a crisis like a crisis. Don't panic; stay calm and very focused. Be clear about the main issue and concentrate on resolving it as speedily and effectively as you can. Keep your mind strictly on what is relevant to sorting things out right now. Above all don't start blaming others or introspecting on why things went wrong. That can wait. If you get involved in that now it will distract you from resolving the crisis. Most crises are not as bad as they appear at first.

Afterwards, reflect carefully on what went wrong and why. Think what you need to do to prevent such a crisis recurring. Unless you change your habits the crisis will probably recur. This is what poor time managers find. Some crises can be put down to external factors largely out of your control but good time planning can help. Sort out the core problem – unrealistic goals, taking on too much, not being able to say no, procrastination or whatever. Any one of these can easily build up into a crisis. Rework your strategy and then plan time to implement it.

A special type of crisis can affect students: being overwhelmed by workload when facing immovable deadlines for essays, exams and so on. The crisis arises through poor time management, combined with a wish to do our very best to get high grades. In such cases, try to renegotiate your workload till you get back on an even keel. Suppose your essay is late because your computer has broken, or your flat has flooded. People understand genuine crises. Don't panic. Explain to your tutor or adviser and its effect on your essay, facing up to why it has happened. You won't be the first student facing this. Ask for an extension and trim your ambitions to what is likely to be practicable.

There are ways of producing acceptable work under crisis conditions which involves 'bare minimum' tactics like restricting the books you use, reading the summary only, getting a basic structure then short notes, bullets which you then expand. While not perfect, this is better than blind panic and can save you from disaster. But do try to monitor such impending crises in advance; face up to reality early.

When you are facing an overwhelming workload remember the four Ds: do, delay, delegate, dump. Decide what has to be done, however well, and what minimum standard is required. Aim for that. If something can be delayed delay it. If you can delegate it or get someone else to do it this will help. Finally you may just be able to dump it. What will really happen if in this instance you don't do it? It's unlikely the world will fall apart. It may just leave you free to focus effectively on other tasks you definitely have to do.

OUTCOMES OF SKILFUL TIME MANAGEMENT

If you take time management seriously, work through and apply the advice offered above what results can you expect? First, you will feel more in control and less guilt. This will give confidence, calmness and a sense of freedom. You certainly won't be wondering where the day went. You'll know you are 'doing all I reasonably can'. You will find you have more tangible, significant achievements and will realise you can learn to cope with the job. You will have a better work/life balance. All this is crucial to being a good teacher and getting satisfaction from your chosen career. It applies equally to being a student in higher education.

You will have begun to build up some significant achievements, small perhaps but important, and they will soon build to bigger ones – a really good essay, set of lessons, presentation. You'll have more focus and gain a reputation for getting things done well and on time.

You'll have a clear defence against workload pressure. From your plan you'll be able to explain why you can't take on more right now or why you need to delay other demands. You'll find you develop clear values and a strong sense from inside your experience of the unhealthy effects of high workload cultures in modern society. You'll have a deeper awareness of the pressures your pupils face as they grow up, especially if the school is dominated by tests and examinations. You will realise that you can be a valuable model and help them learn the same skills for their own lives as pupils and emerging citizens.

APPLYING FOR TEACHER TRAINING

For undergraduate courses whether you are applying while completing school or as a mature student you need to apply through UCAS, the Universities and Colleges Admissions Service (website: www.ucas.co.uk). You can apply online or ask to be sent a form. There is an enormous range of teacher education courses in different universities throughout the UK. It is well worth looking up the details of some courses on the website, or asking for a prospectus from the institutions you are considering, to find the one that most appeals to you.

You will be able to narrow this range significantly as you decide where you want to study. You also need to consider where you would like to teach once qualified since in some cases this may determine where you need to train, for example in England or Scotland. It is important to check out grants and fees before deciding, as there may be significant differences depending on where you reside and where you study.

In the case of postgraduate routes, you have to apply for most courses through the GTTR (www.gttr.ac.uk). These courses are mostly thirty-six-weeks long (four weeks longer than a standard academic year) although there are also a few two-year and some part-time programmes. The regulations for Scotland differ somewhat from those for England and Wales.

If you are considering one of the alternative routes, such as the Graduate Teacher Programme, Advanced Teacher Programme or Teach First, the best approach is through the website www.canteach.co.uk where you will find relevant details. In England and Wales those applying for one-year programmes are eligible for a training salary of £6,000. This does not apply in Scotland.

Whatever programme you are applying for, it is advisable to try to arrange some experience observing in a school first of all. Note that it can take several weeks to receive child protection clearance for working with young people. You usually get in touch with a school in your area or with a school you know through personal contacts or went to yourself. One of the main reasons for obtaining such experience is to make sure you know that you really want to teach and don't just have a romantic notion of what daily life in school is all about. As a classroom observer or helper you can gain an insight into the teacher's role, how schools operate and some experience in interacting with pupils. This should also give you a motivating and confident start to your training course.

For entry to teacher training there is usually an interview and in some cases a more elaborate selection procedure. This is because it is in no one's interest to enrol someone who is clearly not suited or ready for such a course. While some popular courses are difficult to get into, in recent years in both Scotland and England there has been a large demand for teachers.

ACRONYMS, GLOSSARY AND USEFUL WEBSITES

ACRONYMS

(* indicates explanation in Glossary)

ADD	Attention Deficit Disorder
ADHD*	Attention Deficit Hyperactivity Disorder
Cpd*	Continuing professional development
DENI	Department for Education in Northern Ireland
DfEE	Department for Education and Employment
DfES	Department for Education and Skills
EAL	English as an Additional Language
EAZ	Education Action Zone
ICT	Information and Communications Technology
ITE	Initial Teacher Education
ITT	Initial Teacher Training
GNVQ	General National Vocational Qualification
GTCE	General Teaching Council for England
GTCS	General Teaching Council for Scotland
GTCWS	General Teaching Council for Wales
GTP	Graduate Teaching Programme
KS*	Key Stage
LEA	Local Education Authority
LTScotland	Learning and Teaching Scotland
NCC	National Curriculum Council
NFER	National Foundation for Educational Research
NLS	National Literacy Strategy
NQT	Newly Qualified Teacher
Ofsted	Office for Standards in Education
Pbl*	Problem Based Learning

PGCE	Postgraduate Certificate in Education
PGDE	Professional Graduate Diploma in Education (replacing PGCE in Scotland)
PSH	Personal Social and Health Education
QCA	Qualifications and Curriculum Authority
SAT	Standard Assessment Task
SCAA	School Curriculum and Assessment Authority
SCITT	School Centred Initial Teacher Training
SCRE	Scottish Council for Research in Education
SEBD	Social Emotional and Behavioural Difficulties
SEED	Scottish Executive Education Department
SENCO	Special Educational Needs Co-ordinator
TTA	Teacher Training Agency
UCAS	Universities and Colleges Admission Service
VLE	Virtual Learning Environment
Zpd*	Zone of proximal development

GLOSSARY

Accommodation	Developing your framework of thinking to take account of new ideas and experiences.
Action Research	In schools, a research process where insights are developed by changing an aspect of teaching and monitoring the results, sometimes in a continuing cycle of action, monitoring and planning further changes.
ADHD	A disorder which makes it difficult for pupils to sustain attention and inhibit their immediate natural responses.
Assimilation	Building new experiences and ideas into your present network of thinking (schema).
Behaviour modification	Managing behaviour by shaping it using systematic rewards and sanctions.
Behaviourism	Theory of learning focused on overt

behaviours and schedules of
reinforcement, reward and punishment.

Brain gym
Physical exercises and activities designed
to increase attention and involvement in
learning tasks.

Case study
A research study which take an
individual instance as its focus (for
example a class, a group, an individual)
and presents an analysis of some aspect
of their learning – such as their approach
to mental mathematics, reading
difficulties or some more general
theme.

Child centred
A curriculum or teaching based on the
expressed or ascertained needs of the
child in contrast to an adult-imposed
curriculum.

Cognition
Involving memory, attention, perception,
thinking, intelligence, problem-solving.

Cognitive style
Best thought of as a deep-seated, stable
preference for approaching a task or
processing information in a certain way.
Sometimes used interchangeably with
learning style.

Compensation
Recognition that change in one
dimension such as height of water in a
jar can be compensated for by change in
another, for example, width.

Concrete
operations
Piagetian stage (7–11) where children
can solve problems using concrete
objects, for instance counting with
coloured cubes, and can think about two
attributes (like height and weight)
simultaneously. They can now decentre,
and show conservation and
reversibility.

Conservation
task
One which requires the child to watch
the transformation of a substance but not

its basic characteristics, for example water poured into a jar of different height.

Constructivism
A theory about how knowledge is developed and acquired. The claim is that learners actively construct their own knowledge in interaction with the environment and in social interaction – in contrast with the idea that knowledge exists independently of the learner and can be transmitted by some direct means.

Contingent teaching
Teaching where support is provided where learners have difficulties but withdrawn as they show signs of understanding and succeeding on a task.

Continuous professional development
The expectation that teachers will continue to develop professional understanding and skills throughout their career. The system of staff development opportunities and awards which form a ladder of such development opportunities.

Criterion-referenced test
A test comparing performance to a standard (as in a driving test).

Critical thinking
Thinking that is analytic, explanatory and evaluative.

Decentring
The ability to see others' perspectives.

Differentiation
Providing different teaching tasks, support or expectations to match previous attainments and needs of learners.

Dyslexia
A disability in using and interpreting written language and symbols, independent of general intelligence and spoken language skills.

Dyspraxia
A movement impairment which can lead

to problems with language, perception, body awareness and muscle tone.

Early education
Education between birth and eight or three and eight, at one time seen as involving a markedly different curriculum and different teaching approaches to later primary schooling.

Ego-centrism
Apparent lack of awareness that others may have different perspectives.

Emotional intelligence
Awareness of and sensitivity to one's own and others' emotions and ability to express emotions appropriately.

Empirical
Based on and verifiable by observation, experiment and experience.

Evaluation
Analysis and reflection on the quality of teaching, curriculum or some other aspect of education. In American texts evaluation is also used for what in UK is generally called assessment.

Evidence-based practice
Education policies and teaching approaches based on the evidence of systematic (usually large-scale) research studies.

Formal operations
Piagetian stage (eleven onwards) featuring abstract adult thinking. Individuals can consider all possibilities, think ahead, hypothesise and solve problems using abstract symbols as well as concrete objects.

Formative assessment
Assessment designed to help learners by offering feedback, usually during the course of learning. The difference between formative and summative is not in the form or timing of assessment but in its purpose and use. An exam can be formative as well as summative.

Forms of knowledge
Fundamental disciplines such as mathematics, science, history. There are

	thought, in this theory, to be about seven such distinct, basic ways of knowing.
Horizontal décalage	Inability of pupils to master problems requiring the same logical operations but different variables (décalage means gap or discrepancy).
Inclusion	The idea that the ordinary classroom takes in all pupils, whatever their special needs or learning difficulties, offering appropriate curriculum, support and resources as opposed to separating them into special units or schools. Also used to refer to non-discrimination in terms of race, ethnicity, gender, sexuality and social class.
Induction	Post qualifying probationary year for teachers, usually with reduced timetable and guaranteed professional development opportunities and standards for full registration.
Key Stage	In England, Wales and Northern Ireland, stages of the national curriculum programme. The relevant ages are:

Key Stage 1   3–8 years
Key Stage 2   7–11 years
Key Stage 3   11–14 years

Learning outcome	Statement of what learners are expected to have learned by the end of a lesson or course. Objective is an older term for a similar idea.
Learning style	A preferred way of approaching a learning task or receiving information. Often used interchangeably with cognitive style.
Long-term memory	Memory structure which retains items for extended periods of time.
Metacognition	Awareness of one's thinking and thinking strategies.

Modes of teaching	The idea that there are four basic kinds of teaching – direct, action learning, enquiry and discussion. A framework used in several official Scottish educational policy documents since the 1980s.
Multiple intelligences	Theory that intelligence is not confined to a general ability or language and mathematical skills but covers about seven different kinds – including musical, physical, emotional, religious, and inter-personal.
Norm-referenced test	Comparing performances in relation to others' performances, for example a class average or finishing position in a race.
Object permanence	When children show understanding that an object continues to exist even when they cannot see it.
Paradigm	Underlying theories and methods of a subject. A paradigm shift involves a change to the underlying approach and assumptions.
Pedagogy	Theory of teaching approaches. In some contexts, just another word for teaching method. Now widened especially in discussion by sociologists to include assumptions about the nature of knowledge, teaching and learning and assessment.
Pre-operational	Piagetian stage (2–6 years) where children can use symbolic play and language to aid thinking. It is still dominated by perception, children find it difficult to see other's viewpoints, and they have not yet mastered conservation or reversibility.
Professional development portfolio	A folio of selected items to evidence and promote professional development.

Reception class	The first class in an English infant school taking children aged five and sometimes before they reach five.
Reflective practitioner	A teacher who develops by reflecting critically on his or her own practice in the light of relevant theory and practical considerations.
Reinforcement	Verbal or material reward (designed to increase the likelihood of repetition of a behaviour).
Reliability	In essay and exam marking this is best thought of as inter-marker consistency. Marking is reliable if markers independently give the same grade to a script.
Reversibility	Understanding that an action or mental operation can be undone by reversing it (for example by pouring water back into a short, fatter jar).
Scaffolding	Support for learning provided for a learner to make a task easier to accomplish by a teacher or peer (for example by giving hints, breaking down the tasks into manageable sections, or modelling how to proceed).
Schema	A network of ideas or framework of thinking.
Self-esteem	The value we place on ourselves.
Sensori-motor stage	Piagetian stage (0–2 years) where thinking relies on a child's movements and reactions to stimuli in its environment.
Shadow study	An observational study which involves following (shadowing) a pupil around a series of classes or activities.
Short-term memory	Memory structure which can hold only a limited number of items and for a short period.

Situated cognition	The idea that knowledge cannot be separated from the actions that give rise to it or the culture in which actions occur.
Social justice	Equality and absence of discriminatory practice in relation to aspects such as gender, sexual orientation, race, class and ethnicity.
Social learning theory	Learning developed through observation of the behaviour of adult models (developed by A. Bandura).
Spiral curriculum	A curriculum strategy where ideas introduced at one stage are revisited and explored in more depth at a later stage (or stages).
Stage of development	In Piaget's theory a phase of development distinguished from other phases by qualitative differences in thinking.
Standard	In teacher education a statement of expected performance or intended outcome of professional learning – that is, what teachers are expected to know, understand, be able to do, or show commitment to. Standard is a broader notion than competence.
Statementing	Drawing up a formal document describing special needs following assessment with a view to ensuring appropriate resource provision.
Symbolic play	Play in which objects are used to represent other things, for instance a box for a house.
Synthetic phonics	Teaching letter/sound matches and immediately getting students to use this knowledge to read and spell regular words by blending the sounds together – synthesis – hence synthetic phonics.

Target setting	Setting goals in terms of national curriculum levels for individuals and schools in an effort to raise attainment.
Thinking skills	Ability to think logically and creatively and to solve problems.
Transferable skill	A skill which is normally learned in a specific context but which has wider application, such as time management and presentation skills.
Transition	The move from pre-school to primary or primary to secondary schooling. These phases are seen as critical because research has uncovered a hiatus in progression and development at these points for many pupils.
Validity	A test or assessment is valid if it measures what it claims to measure. Testing can have unintended consequences on motivation and opportunities and the term consequential validity is used to take account of these.
Working memory	Another term for short-term memory.
Zone of proximal development	A range of achievement stretching from tasks one can do unaided to what one can achieve with support.

USEFUL WEBSITES

www.behaviour4learning.ac.uk (advice on class management)

www.dfes.gov.uk/ictinschools (ICT ideas)

www.ictadvice.org.uk (ideas for teaching curriculum using ICT)

www.LTScotland.org.uk (Scottish curriculum ideas and materials)

www.nc.uk.net (national curriculum online)

www.qca.org.uk/ca (information on national curriculum and testing)
www.teachingideas.co.uk (lesson plans and ideas)
www.trainee-teacher.co.uk/ (student teacher network)
www.voicecare.org.uk (a voice care network)

BIBLIOGRAPHY

Apple, M. (2004), *Ideology and the Curriculum*, 3rd edn, London: RoutledgeFalmer.

Assessment Reform Group (2002), *Testing, Motivation and Learning*, Cambridge: University of Cambridge Press.

Austin, H., B. Dwyer and P. Freebody (2003), *Schooling the Child*, London: RoutledgeFalmer.

Banks, F., J. Leach and B. Moon (1999), 'New understandings of teachers' pedagogical knowledge' in J. Leach and B. Moon (eds), *Learners and Pedagogy*, London: Paul Chapman.

Barrow, R. (1984), *Giving Teaching Back to Teachers*, Brighton: Wheatsheaf.

Bell, J. (1999), *Doing Your Research Project*, 3rd edn, Buckingham: Open University Press.

Bennett, N. (1976), *Teaching Styles and Pupil Progress*, London: Open Books.

Biggs, J. (2003), *Teaching for Quality learning at University*, 2nd edn, Maidenhead: Open University Press.

Bloom, B. S. (1956 and 1964), *Taxonomy of Educational Objectives*, 2 vols, New York, NY: Longmans Green.

Boud, D, R. Cohen and D. Walker (eds) (1993), *Using Experience for Learning*, Buckingham: Open University Press.

Bricheno, P. and M. Younger (2004) 'Some unexpected results of a learning styles intervention', paper presented to BERA conference Manchester, September, 2004.

Bridges, D. (1978), *Education, Democracy and Discussion*, Windsor: NFER.

Broadfoot, P. (1999), 'Assessment and the emergence of modern society' in B. Moon and P. Murphy (eds), *Curriculum in Context*, London: Paul Chapman, pp. 63–91.

Browne, A. and D. Haylock (2004), *Professional Issues for Primary teachers*, London: Paul Chapman.

Bruner, J. (1960), *The Process of Education*, Cambridge, MA: Harvard University Press.

Bruner, J. (1996), *The Culture of Education*, Cambridge, MA: Harvard University Press.

Burton, D. and S. Bartlett (2005), *Practitioner Research for Teachers*, London: Paul Chapman.

Carr, D. (2000), 'Emotional intelligence, PSE and self-esteem: a cautionary note', *Pastoral Care in Education*, vol. 18, September, pp. 27–33.

Carr, D. (2003), *Making Sense of Education*, London: RoutledgeFalmer.

Cole, M. (ed.) (2000), *Education, Equality and Human Rights*, London: RoutledgeFalmer.

Crème, P. and M. Lea (1997), *Writing at University*, Buckingham: Open University Press.

De Bono, E. (1991) *Six Action Shoes*, London: HarperCollins.

De Bono, E. (2000), *Six Thinking Hats*, London: Penguin.

Deloitte and Touche (2001), *Report of the 'First Stage' Review of Initial Teacher Education, Independent review of the Scottish ITE sector*, Edinburgh: Scottish Executive.

DfES (2003), *Excellence and Enjoyment: a Strategy for Primary Schools*, Nottingham: DfES

Dillon, J. T. (1988), *Questioning and Teaching*, London: Routledge.

Dillon J. T. (1994), *Using Discussion in Classrooms*, Buckingham: Open University Press.

Dixon, A, M. Drummond, S. Hart and D. McIntyre (2004), *Learning without Limits*, Buckingham: Open University Press.

Edwards, A. and J. Warin (1999), 'Parental involvement in raising the achievement of primary school pupils: why bother?' *Oxford Review of Education*, 25: 3, 325–41.

Entwistle, N. (1987), *Understanding Student Learning*, London: Hodder and Stoughton.

Entwistle, N. (1996), 'Recent research on student learning and the learning environment', in J. Tait and P. Knight (eds) *The Management of Independent Learning*, London: Kogan Page.

Entwistle, N. and E. Peterson (2004), 'Learning styles and approaches to studying', *Encyclopedia of Applied Psychology*, 2, 537–42.

Filer, A. and A. Pollard (2000), *The Social World of Pupil Assessment*, London: Continuum.

Fontana, D. (1995), *Psychology for Teachers*, 3rd edn, London: Macmillan.

Friere, A. and D. Macedo (eds) (1998), *The Paulo Friere Reader*, New York: Continuum.

Galton, M. (1999), *Inside the Primary Classroom: 20 Years On*, London: Routledge.

Gardner, H. (1999), 'Assessment in context' in P. Murphy (ed.), *Learners, Learning and Assessment*, London: Paul Chapman.

Giddens, A. (2001), *Sociology*, 4th edn, Cambridge: Polity.

Hayes, D. (2003), *A Student Teacher's Guide to Primary School Placement*, London: David Fulton.

Hayes, D. (2004), *Foundations of Primary Teaching*, 3rd edn, London: David Fulton.

Hoban, G. F. (2002), *Teaching and Learning for Educational Change*, Buckingham: Open University Press.

Jackson, P. (1968), *Life in Classrooms*, Eastbourne: Holt Rhinehart and Winston.

Johnson, S. (2001), *Teaching Thinking Skills*, Philosophy of Education Society of Great Britain.

Joyce, B., E. Calhoun and M. Weil (2000), *Models of Teaching*, 6th edn, Needham, MA: Allyn Bacon.

Kelly, A. V. (2004), *The Curriculum*, London: Sage.

Kolb, D. (1984), *Experiential Learning: Experience as a Source of Learning and Development*, Englewood Cliffs, NJ: Prentice Hall.

Lave, J. and E. Wenger (1991), *Situated Learning: Legitimate Peripheral Participation*, Cambridge: Cambridge University Press.

Macpherson Report (1999), *The Stephen Lawrence Inquiry: Report of an Inquiry by Sir William Macpherson*, London: HMSO.

Mayall, B. (2003), *Sociologies of Childhood and Educational Thinking*, London: Institute of Education, University of London.

McCormick, R and P. Murphy (2000), 'Curriculum', in B. Moon, S. Brown and M. Ben-Peretz (eds), *Routledge International Companion to Education*, London: Routledge.

McNiff, J. (2002), *Action Research: Principles and Practice*, London: Routledge.

Meighan, R. and I. Siraj-Blatchford (1997), *A Sociology of Educating*, 3rd edn, London: Cassell.

Merrett, F. and K. Wheldall (1990), *Positive Teaching in the Primary School*, London: Paul Chapman.

Merttens, R., A. Newland and S. Webb (1996), *Learning in Tandem*, Leamington Spa: Scholastic.

Moore, A. (2000), *Teaching and Learning*, London: Falmer.

Morgan, C., A. Watson and C. Tikly (2004), *Mathematics*, London: RoutledgeFalmer.

Muijs, D. and D. Reynolds (2001), *Effective Teaching*, London: Paul Chapman.

Myers, I. B. and K. C. Briggs (2002), *Myers-Briggs Type Indicator*, http://www.cppdb.com/products/mbti/index.asp

Parkinson, C. N. (1958), *Parkinson's Law: The Pursuit of Progress*, London: John Murray.

Paterson, L. (2003), *Scottish Education in the Twentieth Century*, Edinburgh: Edinburgh University Press.

Powell, J. (1985), *Ways of Teaching*, Edinburgh: Scottish Council for Research in Education.

Pring, R. (1976), *Knowledge and Schooling*, London: Open Books.

Quality Assurance Agency for Higher Education (2000), *The Standard for Initial Teacher Education in Scotland*, Gloucester: QAAHE.

Reeves, J., P. Smith and J. O'Brien (2002), *Performance Management in Education*, London: Paul Chapman.

Roffey, S. (2004), *The New Teacher's Survival Guide to Behaviour*, London: Paul Chapman.

Rogers, W. (2002), *Classroom Behaviour*, London: Paul Chapman.

Scottish Executive (2004), *A Curriculum for Excellence*, Edinburgh: Scottish Executive.

Skinner, B. F. (1968), *The Technology of Teaching*, New York: Appleton

Skinner, D. (1994), 'Modes of teaching', in G. Kirk and R. Glaister (eds), *5–14: Scotland's National Curriculum*, Edinburgh: Scottish Academic Press.

Slater, A. and G. Bremner (2003), *An Introduction to Developmental Psychology*, Oxford: Blackwell.

Stenhouse, L. (1975), *An Introduction to Curriculum Research and Development*, London: Heinemann.

Teacher Training Agency (2002), *Qualifying to Teach: Professional Standards for Qualified Teacher Status and Requirements for Initial Teacher Training*, London: Teacher Training Agency.

Thomas, G. and R. Pring (2004), *Evidence-based Practice in Education*, Maidenhead: Open University Press.

Thompson, N. (1998), *Promoting Equality: Challenging Discrimination and Oppression in the Human Services*, London: Macmillan.

Tinklin, T. and D. Raffe (1999), *Entrants to Higher Education*, Edinburgh: Centre for Educational Sociology.

Weissmann, J. and B. Kaszubski (2004), *Absolute Beginner's Guide to Winning Presentations*, Indianapolis: QUE.

Wragg, E. and G. Brown (2001a), *Questioning in the Primary School*, London: RoutledgeFalmer.

Wragg, E. and G. Brown (2001b), *Explaining in the Secondary School.* London: RoutledgeFalmer.

INDEX